Other Books by Vesper Hunter:

A Head on my Shoulders (1985), 17th C.,
Pure Madness, (1986) 17th C.,
Best Second Best (1987) 20th C.,
Jacon (1989) 19th C.,
The Hills are Alive (Editor) 1988 (Local interest)

I am grateful to John Reilly for so generously allowing his paintings to be reproduced in this book

Vesper Hunter

BELOVED BROTHER

Vesper Hunter
2.12.93

Vesper Hunter

A Square One Publication

First published in 1993 by
Square One Publications
Saga House, Sansome Place, Worcester, WR1 1UA

© Vesper Hunter 1993

ISBN: 1 872017 76 2

British Library Cataloguing in Publication Data
is available for this book

Typeset by Avon Dataset, Bidford-on-Avon, Warwickshire B50 4JH
Printed in Great Britain by Antony Rowe Ltd, Chippenham, Wiltshire

Contents

Foreword

I was determined to find this young man! Where was the 'Arabia' to which he had fled, and where he had disappeared without trace for approximately three years? He had been known as Rabbi Saul of Tarsus and then, at his own request, was re-named Paul, and later, because canonised, he became familiar, slightly off-putting, as 'Saint' Paul.

As an older man he can certainly be held responsible for the spread of the Christian religion throughout the world and down the centuries. Yet, whilst undoubtedly a great teacher, preacher, scholar, writer, he emerges for me as a rather elderly, person, dogmatic, authoritarian, anti-feminist, highly intellectual, kindly, but speaking in an old-fashioned, classical way that seems irrelevant to the everyday life, noise and confusion of the 20th century. There is more here than a generation gap!

He had great adventures, shipwrecks, lynchings etc., and though he wrote movingly of love, he could never have survived today without much more to him than that! I never felt I knew him. Preachers and teachers have dragged him through their minds until I cannot recognise a personality behind their thought. Useless to look in the churches, in that forest of dead wood and tangled undergrowth, for a living man. Anyway, I was not looking for that older Paul whose letters have survived to today, but for the younger man who had so shamelessly, and almost overnight, changed from being a fanatical, hot-headed young Jew, to being one of the rebels he had so ardently determined to exterminate, and one more devoted to their Leader than any of them.

Was it because he was so stunned by his complete change of direction that he went off 'to Arabia' for approximately three years? Perhaps! Since we hear no more of him during that time.

What did he do in those years? What happened to him? Which 'Arabia?'

I had followed the steps of the older Paul in Israel, Turkey, Greece, and Cyprus. That had been an historical pilgrimage, but this search was quite different. This was an imaginative, spiritual journey and I travelled with the young Paul through Jordan, to the 'Arabia' of his day and came to know, love and understand him and finally share his devotion to the cause of Love, to which he gave his life.

I wrote his Journal as we travelled together, and marvelled at the experiences through which he learned and grew as a result of that rich encounter on the Damascus road, which so changed his life.

Vesper Hunter

Preface

Nearly two thousand years after it was written, Paul's journal is released to us. He prefaces it with a letter, extracts from which are necessary reading for the understanding of the events the journal records.

From Paul, beloved of God and brother of our Lord, Jesus, to all citizens of the Kingdom, lovers of my Lord — Greeting!

I, Paul, leave to you all this journal, written in my own hand during the two years when I was in Arabia after my Lord first revealed himself to me and when I bound myself to him for ever . . .

. . . You will know from my letters to you, which I know are still read among you, how constantly I referred in them to my unworthiness of God's love, for I, the last and least of the apostles, persecuted those first lovers of Jesus without mercy. Yet he, who himself was despised, rejected and condemned to crucifixion under the Law, neither despised nor rejected me, nor judged me guilty of his death though I was under the Law that condemned him. He came to me when I was at the height of my anger and jealousy of him and his followers and he won my allegiance and devotion with his love for me, a love springing from Love Itself . . .

. . . Before you read the journal I must tell you of that first and blessed encounter. I was journeying to Damascus a few weeks after his crucifixion, armed with letters from the Sanhedrin giving me authority to exterminate his followers by any method I chose . . .

. . . We had left Jerusalem for Damascus well before daybreak. The sky was starlit when we left, with a bright sickle moon and we had a five hour journey before us. We had journeyed for about two hours and darkness was fading as our road turned sharply to the east where dawn would soon break. There were four of us travelling on horseback. One of my companions was a retired member of the Temple guard and the other two were servants of the old High Priest, Annas, who had generously lent them to me. I was impatient to reach the end of my journey so we had travelled swiftly from Jerusalem. My companions did not know me well and were in considerable awe of this wild, young, fanatical Doctor of the Law, going at speed to Damascus, an envoy from the Sanhedrin. It was, in fact, the Sanhedrin who had hired them and paid them to escort me, so they also felt a sense of privilege, having been chosen for an important job.

My thoughts on the journey were uninterrupted. I was still smarting over the loss of my friend Stephen's love and bitter about his death. I felt desperately alone and unsure of myself. What was I? Who was I? — This angry, jealous, hurt, virile, young man! A first class Jewish scholar? Yes, but wandering as any nomad in search of a promised land. An exile from my true home? But where was my true home? A murderer? — For I had committed murder. Or was I a religious fanatic refusing to accept that I was merely a frustrated secret lover, doomed for ever to a fruitless search for fulfilment? I did not know how to see myself for I could not, in honesty, accept any one of these roles. None fitted the reality of my every day. In a vague way, the only role in which I had confidence was that I knew myself a child of some Creator — as such, a dismal failure — but still struggling to understand and fulfil that role.

I conducted a monologue with myself on that road. One day, I realised, I must reach a point where I accepted myself honestly, either as son of Adam, the natural man, or a diligent follower of Moses and the Law. Or was I a child of faith, floundering in loving obedience to God as Abraham had done? I know now, as I look back, that, out of envy, I was fighting the people of the Way, those followers of Jesus of whom Stephen had been one. Deep down I longed to have the courage to be one of them, to share the joy and freedom that they seemed to have found through their love of their leader. In my jealousy of them I hated them and was proud that I had been given the privilege of the journey to Damascus with authority to exterminate them.

We had just climbed a long hill, the highway winding steadily up and round the shoulder and we had wondered whether we would see Damascus from the crest, none of us having travelled that way before. I had called to the men, 'Stop in the next wadi and we will take food!' And they had galloped ahead and then called to me that it was a suitable place. I caught up with them, reined in my horse, dismounted and they led her down to the water.

They were slow and I was impatient with them for they would not make haste. The earth under my feet felt hard, rocky and unreal. The sky seemed more real as a pale light dispersed the dawn mist and spread across the eastern horizon. I watched it change gently, surely, in merging bands of cream, apricot and ochre, like rolling sands of another world. Beyond that heavenly desert, stretching beyond the horizon's edge was a wide sea of deepest blue and beyond again were distant mountains of dark cloud.

Then it happened. The sun rose suddenly in flame and a pathway of pure and shining light streamed across that heavenly world to my feet and I heard a voice. "Saul," It said, "Saul, why do you fight against me?" Brilliant light flooded around me and eclipsed the wadi, the men, the horses, the world. I was alone, enveloped in Light and dazzled by it.

"Lord, Who are you?" I heard myself shout and the Light beyond the horizon blazed more brightly as the sun rose in orange and flame and fiery scarlet and crimson and at its heart I saw the dead body of the man, Jesus, hanging on that cross. The crimson turned scarlet like blood and then changed back to flame and orange and the pathway shone in pure and blinding light and in that Light I saw that same man, alive, a man moving towards me, a man beloved before time began, god from God, light from Light, truly man, truly God,

"I am Jesus, whom you persecute! Why would you crucify me?" He said. He reached out to me and drew me to him and held me close in that world of Light.

"It is hard for you, Saul, my brother, to kick against the pricks, of conscience, of pride, of falsehood and deceit. I am the Way, the Truth and the Life. Love freely, my brother, as I love you. You are made in the image of Love and Love is the One God over all gods, above all and in you all. This is the way and truth and life I lived among you, and now I call you, beloved brother, to bear witness to Love in my name. Believe in me! Trust me! Live in love with me and, through me, in love with all humanity. Throughout every moment of your life, with loving care, Love has led you to this moment, to bear witness to His Power."

Silence fell. Time stood still . . .

. . . I do not know how long it was before he released me. The Light dispersed and spread to form the light of a new day. The path faded. I felt again the earth under my feet, hard, rocky and unreal. I was back on the edge of the wadi, groping, totally blinded by the Light of that world into which I had been newly born. I neither heard nor saw anything but, in Light and in Love, I knew, as never before, who I was and for what I was made. I had found a depth in me, an unconscious dimension, unknown before, that, when brought to the Light was a profound reality that lay behind, above, within the everyday world. Not in it; not out of it; but with it. All my laboured learning, my hasty struggling, my easy self-love and pious self-chastisement I saw as pathetic human endeavour. My efforts had been of no avail until they were made one by this man, this Jesus, whom I knew was now and for ever my true and only Lover.

Have I caught that revelation for you in words? How else can I reveal it? Now that that day is many years ago, how do I see it? As vision? Fantasy?

Reality? Symbol? Whether in the body or out of the body, I know not. But this I know, that I was drawn into the heavens and that it is an experience more vivid to me than any other I have had on earth. It is real beyond dream or vision. Without being embraced by Love I would have had no gospel to give you, no experience of the mortal putting on immortality, or of the spirit giving life to the body. Jesus is Lord, brother, lover, of us all; reuniting each of us with Love, our Father and Creator. This is the way of Christ. We are his Body. The Love that is God is revealed in every touch given or received and every word spoken in his name. No argument, theological discourse, understanding or explanation of any law is needed to make this clear. Only Love can reveal it in life and Love's most profound symbol is seen in Jesus Christ, crucified and alive again . . .

. . . What of all my mistakes, failures, wrongdoings? How they had haunted me and what guilt I carried before I knew my Lord Jesus. They are no more to be judged than my achievements, successes or good deeds. They have all been caught up in the light of Love. Whether forgiven or accepted I neither know nor care. They are all part of Love's creation.

Nevertheless, as you know from my earlier letters, I boast! Not in my achievements, for they are no boasting matter, but − I boast in that I am beloved of God and in this I rejoice. It is the ground of my confidence, my faith, my hope, my love − his love for me and mine for him . . .

. . . My journal was written many years before any of my letters to you, when I was an inexperienced young man in Arabia between my two visits to

Damascus. My first visit there followed immediately after that first encounter of which I have told you and which so changed my life. The second visit was prior to my final return across Jordan river to begin the work for which Love had been so surely preparing and commissioning me. I was to spread to the whole world the good news of Love as I had received it from my Lord, for he is Messiah, Christ, Saviour, of all mankind. This was my calling for as far and as long as my life-time on earth would permit. This I have faithfully done and I know that the truth of Love I preach through Jesus, the Christ, reaches beyond space, beyond time, into the realm of spirit which has no boundaries and where, beloved brothers and sisters, you too, now, live with me in Christ, Whenever, wherever, my journal is read, in this world of spirit, I meet and greet you with the blessing of Love, God above all gods, the Father of us all. To Him be glory and thanksgiving for ever and ever, throughout all worlds and throughout all ages. Amen.

"ENLIGHTENMENT" - Oil - 36" x 48" - John Reilly

After Damascus

I am to-day beginning a journal.

Days and events since my Lover won my allegiance have taken on new meaning. My life before that day had been one of unmitigated hunger and unabated struggle, to keep the Law and be worthy of the forgiveness and mercy of God and also be true to myself. Life was charged with guilt, sin and furtive failure, Now, every day's events, all contacts, however seemingly trivial, are Love's gift to me. Life is illuminated and I must record what is happening and what has happened.

Passover time is here again. Several weeks ago I was determined to go back to Jerusalem, find acceptance with my Lord's friends and become one of them so that together we might celebrate the anniversary of his death. How strange and surely joyful that celebration would have been as we recalled the apparent disaster of his crucifixion turned to joy when they knew him to be alive. Then I would have recalled how my hatred of them all was now turned to love and I would tell them that I, too, knew him to be alive. I would be accepted as one of them for he was their friend as he was my lover. How wrong I was to imagine things could have come about like that. As a result of what happened I am here, only two day's journey from Damascus, still east of Jordan, in the hills somewhere near the wadi where, three months ago I had come face to face with

1

my true and eternal lover and where my union with him took place.

When I reached the ford a week ago to cross over Jordan and make for Jerusalem my feet were turned away. Clearly I heard my Lord say, "Not yet!" So I turned back, thankfully, for I knew I was not yet ready to return. I need more time, carefully, honestly, to find out what took place at that wadi, on that day and how I am to follow and serve Jesus, my Lord and Lover.

That night I slept alone under the stars and again had my strange, so often recurring, dream of my battle in life. How often dreams and visions have been part of my life and truth has been revealed to me by their means but, this time, while I was still battling I knew the war was over.[*] Love and Light had won and I was on the side of the Victor and the Victor was my Lover, Jesus, the Christ. It instantly became clear to me that I could not go back to either Tarsus or Jerusalem until I fully understood how I was to serve my Lord and how live my love for him.

So here I am now and have been here over a week with this warm and welcoming family, sharing their tent and their life and gratefully accepting their hospitality.

"You are welcome, brother," Naboth had said, when I caught up with them. "You passed us by the ford yesterday, just after we crossed over. Your face was turned towards Jerusalem. Have you changed your mind?"

The separate parchment on which Paul wrote his dream was found at the end of his journal and is entered as an Appendix to this book.

"I dreamed a strange dream, my friends," I replied, "and it is this that has altered my plans." "Before long," I continued to Naboth, "I expect to continue my journey from Damascus to join my friends in Jerusalem, but the time is not yet."

I had hesitated, wondering whether I would ask for hospitality but before I could do so, Naboth, who, it was clear, was the father and leader of this Bedouin group, had said, "Dreams and portents must not be ignored, brother. He who closes his mind to their meaning can all too easily lose his way, whether on the journey of his soul through life or whether he is finding his way by the stars through the desert. Stay with us, brother, and share our food and shelter until the morning. By then, perhaps, your way will be clear."

I gladly accepted his invitation and have stayed with them since that evening.

I raise my pen and think long . . . I cannot find words to describe my experience on the road to Damascus. It needs no record other than in my heart and I myself am as yet without full understanding. The facts are easy and if their meaning is true as I believe it is, I have found, after a lifetime of searching, longing, hungering, the goal and purpose of my life. This is no longer to struggle with the Law, hoping to find in its fulfilment the way to live the good life but it is to know myself united with the Love Who created me. Love is my God and that God was revealed to me by Jesus in his love shown to me in a wadi near Damascus.

While my pen was at rest young Reuben shyly entered my corner of the tent. It is a corner made mine and accepted as mine by all the household of the camp. He came to call me to the evening meal of bread dipped in sheep's broth with cheese and dates. Their broth was delicious, mixed with cumin and herbs that were new to me.

I rose and joined the men who had returned with the goats and sheep and who, having fed the camels, shared their meal with me. Young Reuben sat by his father whose arm circled him as he fed him choice morsels from the dish. From the trust in Reuben's eyes and the joy and pride in his father's I knew it was not just food they shared but, much more deeply, they shared the love I had been given by my Lord and Lover.

Two weeks ago I left Damascus ignominiously. I was loth to leave but I had been misunderstood by so many. The elders of the Damascus synagogue had been shocked when they learned that I, their greatest supporter, was living with the people of the Jesus Way.

At first, when living with Judas in Straight Street and later, when I was seen with Ananias, Crispus and both Jewish and Gentile followers of my Love, many suspected that I was using the subtle tactics of a spy, feigning sand-blindness and that my aim was to infiltrate the Jesus people and pin-point the traitors to the synagogue so that my arrests might be of the ring-leaders and real renegades. How could they be anything other than, at first, bewildered and then angry? Suspicion of me grew until they were forced to realise that my words were not a disguise but were with sincerity and conviction. Jesus was my life and my faith and nothing would separate me from the love I had found in him. Both sides had heard the story of that morning on the road to Damascus. The servants who had been with me on the journey had told them before they had returned to Jerusalem a few days later. They had been very frightened by what had happened. They had seen the bright light, 'like a curtain of flame', which, they said, had terrified both them and the horses. When it had passed and they came to me they said I was writhing on the ground, my hands over my eyes, saying, 'My Love, My Love'. My pack and wallet had fallen down the wadi and they retrieved them and then waited until I was quieter. They had helped me to my feet and I had groped, speechless, and could find neither rein nor saddle and as far as they could tell the light had blinded me. So they had led me anxiously to the city and to Judas, the apothecary, in Straight Street who, they were told, would take me in and probably treat my condition. I remember nothing of the journey, nothing of the house in Straight Street, little of the apothecary at that time, though later he was to become a friend. I only dimly remember quiet feet going to and fro, offering me drink and food which I was unable to eat. I was totally held by my Lover and the world was dead to me. Later I was told that the letters in my wallet, sealed and clearly addressed to the synagogue elders in Damascus had been delivered and so it was known that I had come in order to exterminate or imprison those who followed the Jesus Way.

After several days, perhaps as much as a week, came the first visit of Ananias. He came for a reason I did not then understand, though later he told me. As soon as he touched me I knew he trusted me and then I found he had been sent to me by my Lord. It was Ananias' trust in me, his recognition that I was a beloved brother, and his acceptance of me, that brought me back to earth. I saw the world clearly again and found myself face to face with the brethren. I felt their warmth as I touched hand or arm and all around me were their kind, anxious eyes but their smiles were cautious as I took food from them. Then I recognised, in many of them, too, fear and apprehension. Women covered their faces as I passed and children ran away, screaming. I look back now and marvel at the courage of Brother Ananias in coming to see me. He had known my reputation in Jerusalem for he was one who left for Damascus after Stephen's death, not knowing, of course, that Stephen was my friend. He had heard, as they all had, of the contents of the letters that I had brought with me. He must have wondered whether he had fled from Jerusalem only to be pursued to Damascus and fall straight into the hands of the worst of the persecutors of the Way. But, no. It was Love that brought Ananias to me. Never for one moment did he doubt or suspect me.

One evening, soon after his first visit to me and before the sun set at the commencement of the Sabbath, Ananias and I went down alone to a small stream that flowed into the Abana river and there he baptised me. How easily my thoughts stray when I remember that moment. They say that a drowning man sees every moment of his life vividly before his eyes before he is finally swallowed up by the waters. It was like that for me and it was partly to symbolise that, that I allowed Ananias to baptise me and so initiate me into that group of believers. He had told me that baptism was being increasingly used as a sign by which the followers of Jesus made known their membership of the Way. I let him baptise me for I was ready to do anything to prove that I was one who knew Jesus was alive as much as any of them. I went down into the water. As it flowed over me, I felt it cleansing, enfolding, accepting me and I came out a new man, hearing my Lord's words ringing clearly — "You are my beloved brother. You are washed over by Love and this Love which you now know I have freely given to you always."

No longer was the fear and shame of my old life-style and envy of the freedom of Jesus' friends driving me to destroy them. I saw them through Love's eyes and as they asserted that he, their Lord, was alive, so now did I. More than them all I knew him and had met him face to face in the Way. Surely my baptism would convince them of my sincerity. Yet wheresoever and to whomsoever I spoke of my Lord I sensed distrust, hesitancy and suspicion. Many of his followers had fled from Jerusalem to Damascus, as Ananias had done and many stories among us were becoming distorted as they passed from mouth to mouth, though there were also many who had seen my Lord alive. Rumour and gossip were mixed with truth. Only Ananias stood by me. I was myself in confusion and my feelings — despair, pain, frustration, anger and longing — aroused as never before. Love was demanding an allegiance and single-minded devotion, a clarity of thinking and an unswerving direction of will in the midst of so much suspicion and distrust. After several weeks I realised I needed to go back to Jerusalem to meet those who had been closest to my Lord in his life-time. I had to make myself known as one of them and I had much to learn from them. I admit I was afraid. How could I face Gamaliel, Nicodemus, Caiaphas and the Sanhedrin? On the other hand how could I avoid them? How could I stay longer in Damascus when I caused so much distress and argument and was finding myself increasingly unacceptable? Where could I go?

The brethren in Jerusalem have innumerable proofs that Jesus is alive. Some of his closest friends, some just simple tradesmen and some from Galilee, are now, we have heard, transformed by his spirit of Love and are emerging as leaders. Could I convince them that I, their former persecutor, knew my Lord as well as they did? I, who had never had the chance to eat and drink and walk and talk with him daily, as they had before his crucifixion? Yet, I am one of them and now with great and sure insistence my Lord is making clear to me that the love he gives to me is God's Love and is not for me alone but for every member of the human race and he needs me to spread this Love.

Finally the day came when Ananias and I realised I would have to leave Damascus and return to Jerusalem. How I bless that man. Whenever we talked together I knew such peace and trust and openness between us and we knew this was the spirit of Jesus, of Christ, of Love, alive, in and with each of us, giving us clear direction.

Ananias came to the gate with me when I set off. I joined the merchants, tradesmen, shepherds, farmers, a camel caravan and country people returning home, donkeys laden with purchases from Damascus market and even a posse of Roman soldiers marching off to some out-post or some building project. For a week I journeyed, my steps getting slower. Then, the night before I reached Jordan river, I dreamed my dream again. This time I found myself fighting firmly on the side of Light and against the darkness and my Lord Jesus spoke clearly and surely – "In my light, Paul, you will see Light. In my love you know Love. But not yet to

Jerusalem. I have much to teach you. The time to cross is not yet."

My dream and those repeated words have made it clear that I am not ready for Jerusalem. Oh, with what clarity he is showing me this! "Not yet to Jerusalem!" In amazement I hear him. It is no longer human fear that holds me back but an insistent calling, heard and not yet understood, to go beyond the Great Sea to the Gentiles. I am ready to go but not prepared. So I have arranged to stay with this Bedouin family here in the hills and they have welcomed me for as long as I wish.

I am on the fringe of unbelievable insights into the heart and mind of Love through my union with Jesus, my lover and this marvel is for all Love's children, brothers and sisters of Christ, children of one Father. Because of the immensity of this recognition I will stay this side of Jordan for however long it is necessary for me to think through and understand the length and depth and height of this Love which passes all understanding, feeling, imagination. Then and only then will I return, first to Jerusalem, then to wherever Love will direct.

It is near dawn as I write, my friends are sleeping around me. Old Naboth is snoring in the corner by the donkey. My oil is running low and my flame guttering but I know that I must write of all these things, my life-story I suppose, for I must clear my thought, review my mind, look deep into my heart. The old Law with its struggle and demands has passed away. All things are new, so new. From that moment when I met him, I have not lived alone, for he lives in me, not as I was or will be but as I am. My past has brought me to him and my past life is hidden with him in Love Who made me.

Does my story unfold backward from that day of revelation? Or does it unroll from my birth to the day of that meeting with my lover? I am not writing my autobiography. I am struggling to recollect every experience of my life and see each one before and after in the light of that day, as part of the revelation of Eternal Beauty that I saw in him and that transfigures my life. Little wonder the revelation blinded me! All I had seen of life through human eyes was suddenly lost, in deepest darkness, eclipsed by the Light of Love in the eyes of that man on the edge of the wadi.

We had stopped to water the horses though the stream was nearly dry. The men scrambled down the slope with them and I was left at the top looking down. My mind was a ferment of hatred, of jealousy, of frustration, as, wanting the journey over, I saw the men unhurriedly squatting on their haunches while I was impatient to reach Damascus. I wanted to get down to the business of hunting out those who had fled after Stephen had died. I had loved Stephen. God knows how I loved him and he loved me. But after he met the Nazarene he changed. "Saul," he had said, "this man is different from any of the men we have ever known. He loves us but he never loses sight of himself as beloved son of God, his Father. He loves us, not just as men but as beloved children of the same Father. He sees nothing apart from Love and he sees himself and us in the light of Love, made in his Father's image, Love's image, beloved. There is a dignity in his concept of mankind that you and I have never known, for Love is his God. He is, without doubt, Messiah, Christ, the One we have longed for, who has overthrown the kingdoms of this world, not by conquest or military might but by bringing us to life in the spiritual kingdom of Love. We are sons of God and, as such, we all are brothers. Saul, can you not see this?''

Much more he said and it was all nonsense and bitterness to me. My training as a Pharisee had convinced me that the fulfilling of the Law was the only way for a Jew to reach the Kingdom. There was no other way. Yet, behind this intellectual acceptance and mental discipline I had tried to stifle that other love I had known — that other man in me whose human desires had led me into the world of those young men of Tarsus with whom I had known such delight, such satisfaction of human hungers and such passionate loving.

These followers of the Nazarene — not just Stephen but others amongst them, even Roman soldiers and god-fearers, as well as the gang of uncouth young countrymen down from Galilee — these people were the ones I would crush. This seemed especially urgent in the days after the Nazarene's death when they had become even more vociferous with the claim that he had never been killed by crucifixion but was being seen, alive and well, amongst them. Stephen had deserted me and was now dead and I was haunted still by the scene I had watched as he was stoned. I was haunted, too, by that dead and bloody wreckage of the man I had seen hanging on the cross. His followers were licentious, all of them, self-indulgent and completely unrestrained. Though they were totally nonconforming yet it was hard to pin down their law-breaking and blasphemy for they were daily in the Temple, singing the old chants, fulfilling the rituals. But they had, as well, a sense of abandon and joy that I had never, never thought to see in the Temple precincts. I was jealous, envious and full of scorn.

All these thoughts and memories were seething in me as the horses shifted thirstily in the wadi, finding a trickle of water here and another there and I, longing to continue our journey.

Then, it happened. That voice, the Light and then the blindness. "Why, in God's Name, are you persecuting me? Why? Why? Why?" And that word rumbled and cracked like thunder round me and is still echoing in my ears.

I am still with Naboth and his family. Have been busy with tent repairs with no time to write until this evening, two weeks later. I must try to discipline myself and systematically recall and retell the events of my life that led up to that moment at the wadi. I must write carefully of each stage of my life's journey to this point for, though still confused, I see now that it is not a series of fragmented episodes strung together over thirty years but a creative, gradually unfolding, tapestry, with a pattern ordered and unique. At the end, or rather, at this moment, it is incomplete and unfinished, but its design is clear in the Mind of my Maker as the finished carpet was always clear to the weaver. At the end it is neither carpet nor cloth that is made, but I, Paul, who will stand revealed before my God, flawless and complete as He, in Love, made me.

Abila – One Month Later

I must recall first in detail those days before the Passover last year. As I write I find it hard to believe that it is I, Paul, about whom I write. I knew the man, Saul, well, yet he is dead, and I am alive, and it is strange to find myself writing objectively about those days. I was more totally involved in the persecution of the Jesus men than anyone else. My fiery nature was totally caught up with the trapping of these people, pin-pointing their Law-breaking and blasphemy. I hated them deeply. I watched them, living as I longed to live, more close to each other than brothers, really loving each other in open warmth, arms across shoulders, hands held long and sure, eyes dancing in each other's. I watched them one evening come down a staircase from an upper room in a house near the wall, where they seemed often to congregate. They were just laughing together, voices ringing out in free delight. Then often again I watched them, quietly together, accepting, undemanding, unpossessive. How I hated them for they had found what I longed for, free friendship in love together, fearless, guiltless. They were in the Temple often, praising God, joining in psalm-singing and chanting, knowing all the ritual but apparently oblivious and untroubled when they slipped up or 'broke' traditions. I never actually saw Jesus among them. Jerusalem is a large city, teeming with locals and strangers, folk from the country and foreigners, especially at Passover time. In its narrow streets even near neighbours may never meet till all goes back to normal when the feast is over. There were increases of Roman militia in the city and Herodian guards in the Temple at these times, for uproars from small factions were not infrequent — racist, political, fanatical, with youthful radicalism which easily flared up and needed restraint.

It was even easier for me, when Jerusalem was so crowded, to escape to the barracks, where, speaking Greek and in the casual dress of the old Tarsus days — so much more comfortable and familiar than when I was robed as a good, conforming Pharisee in fringe and philacteries — I would drink and play the fool with the soldiers whose company I so much enjoyed and where love could be made surreptitiously, with secrecy if not without fear. I enjoyed both the secrecy and the fear and the Pharisees were too busy with preparations and observances for the feast, and the Sanhedrin too busy with committees and political intrigue to miss one young, normally diligent and scholarly Pharisee.

On the night of his capture I had been at the soldiers' club, dicing, gambling, disguised in the dress of any down-town citizen, outside the barracks beyond the Kedron valley. It was not until noon on the following day that I heard of his arrest. I came out of hiding, dressed again in Pharisee's regalia and was speedily welcomed as I turned my mind back to the business of doing all I could to exterminate this Jesus crowd, this country rabble, with their following of dubious women. Soon I was told that Jesus himself, posing as a Jewish king and being hailed by many as a god, had been summarily arrested by a Herodian guard, caught red-handed with his gang. I shrugged my shoulders and went up to the Temple to pray with the strictest of my class and with all our talk being of the correct observance of the minutiae of the Law that the preparations for Passover demanded. It seemed to me that we were coming out well from the arrest of the Galilean imposter. He who is now my Leader, my lover, my Lord! But then I felt at one with the Sanhedrin, the Herodians, Roman law, Pilate — we all had won a victory. So had I, for I had returned to my rôle as promising young scholar, Gamaliel's top pupil, Master of the Law and another night at the club undetected.

I can remember my sneering hatred which covered my longing for acceptance. It seems impossible that it was to be only a few weeks later that that leader would have claimed me as his beloved and that I would be his for ever and he my Lord and Christ. "I am Jesus whom you persecute!" had been his first words to me. "Why?" He had asked me. Did he mean that he felt at one with the poor, simple fellows I had had arrested? Those country men I had had flung into the dungeons with their noisy bawling and uncontrolled laughter, their stories of the miraculous feeding of crowds and the healing of individuals and even the raising of someone from death? "Why persecute me?" He had said. But at that moment I knew, and I know it as I write now, that I was the persecuted, hacking my way through a thicket of thorns. "It is hard for you to kick against the pricks!" He had said.

How easily I stray from my record of the facts. As I write I know the man I was is dead and I am alive — a new man because I am loved. As I re-read this parchment I cannot but pause to marvel at what, in one way, seems my transformation and yet is really my transfiguration. For I am unchanged. I am the same being, born thirty years ago, a Jewish boy, in Tarsus. All that I have done, been, experienced has enabled me to realise now what I am, applying my heart, mind and will to the meaning of my life. The Law can take me, manipulate me, judge me right or wrong but it cannot change me. God has made me in His image and I can be no other. I am beloved by Jesus, my risen master. I have seen and know him and he has shown me the depths and heights of the Love that is God. Sin has no more meaning for or dominion over me. I an Love's servant, prisoner and lover for ever.

Again my thoughts stray. When I realised that Jesus had been actually condemned and led out to his death my mind flew at once to Stephen. It would hit him hard and I must visit him. Perhaps now, with the imminent death of his new lover, he would be mine again. I had pushed my way out of the Temple courtyard, into the market area and I heard plenty of comments about the last days and pieced the story together. The Sanhedrin had once again been up against Pilate and he had been vacillating as usual. He had liberated old rascal Barabbas as a gesture to celebrate the Passover and the trial and judgement of Jesus had been a thoroughly bogus and put up affair, with Pilate having his usual language problem, distrusting inadequate translators and washing his hands in front of everyone as some sort of dumb charade. They seemed to be unable to find any crime that Jesus had committed that was worthy of death but he had said things that were tactless and blunt and so he was labelled as a blasphemer by extremists on the Council. It made me still more troubled for Stephen who had got himself so unnecessarily caught in this rabble. I went back into the Temple for the mid-day prayers, feeling, in a guilty way, that I must show myself a worthy rabbi and watch my steps. I had no wish at that moment to run into or ally myself in any way with the trouble-makers of either side. I would make it clear that I was an upholder of the Law and still Gamaliel's top scholar.

Prayers over, I pushed again out of the Temple precincts and through to the Old City to Stephen's house outside Herod's gate. I found him under the old fig tree in his courtyard. He was alone, his head in his hands and I sat beside him on the edge of the well. He did not look up and appeared not to know that anyone had come near. I put my hand on his knee and he lowered a hand on to mine. It was wet with tears. For some time we sat silently and then he began.

"I worshipped that man," he said. "I've had many lovers, Paul, as you well know, but this man was different. Amongst the strong he was the strongest; amongst the weak, the weakest. He loved us more than any of us loved him and he accepted the scorn and ridicule and hatred of mankind with pride and dignity. He separated no one from himself and yet he was alone. Yet he was never alone for all the goodness and beauty and truth that is Love shone in him and on us when we were with him. Yet evil men have risen up all round him to slay him. The Council was caught in the evil as were Herod's soldiers. So was Pilate. So were the people. So were we, for those of us who were closest to him left him and ran for our lives in fear. I watched the soldiers march him back from Pilate's judgement hall. Blood ran down his back and his arms and legs and face for they had whipped him. I could stand no more. Paul, he is as good as dead. The Light of Life has gone out for ever and I have nothing to live for except the memory that I have known Love in human form and he loved me."

He buried his head in his hands and great sobs shook him; I could say and do nothing to reach or ease that pain. He had beautiful hands. I loved that young man. What use was that?

Sometime later a woman from the house came with a dish of olives and figs and grapes and some bread and cheese. We idled with the food and Stephen became quieter and less tense. Only time could soften his grief and I rose to go.

The sun would soon set and feeling myself shaken and drained by Stephen's grief I hardly noticed where I went, but walked outside and round the City wall and found I was passing the pauper's burial ground and near the place where crucifixions take place, I am not sure what drew me. I gave little conscious thought to where or why I went but I was climbing up a hill slope noticing tiny marigolds and scarlet anemones in the grass at my feet and small clumps of pennywort in the crevices of wall and rock. They were unaware of and insensitive to human pain. Vultures were flying in the sky as I turned round the huge rock near the hill-top. As I looked up I saw him. I was right at the foot of three crosses, a dead body hanging from each of them. The central one was Stephen's friend, Jesus, for they had pinned a caption on the cross, a mockery calling him a King. A Roman centurion challenged me. I replied in Latin, jesting, "Can't even take a stroll in these

parts but you guys are waiting to string us up!" My
voice sounded cracked and taunting. Before I turned
to go I looked again at the Galilean. What a man he
must have been before death — tall, supple, strong,
under the blood that caked his wounds and spattered
his skin. His head, with a rough crown of thorns set
at a crazy angle on it, had dropped forward on his
chest. He was young, about the same age as I — a
good-looking fellow, healthy, firm muscled but dead,
now, without a doubt. I shuddered, never before
having had reason to study a dead body on a cross. It
was gruesome and I knew it was a miscarriage of
justice. I remembered Stephen's tears which had
been tears for his living lover, not this dead
wreckage here. I turned, called good-night to the
guard and went, passing a small band of Jews,
officials, who greeted me. I recognised amongst
them a man called Joseph, whom I knew slightly, a
friend of Gamaliel's, I think. What had brought him
and his friends up that hill on that night, I
wondered. But what had brought me? I had to hurry
down for the sun would soon be setting and there
were great clouds about after unusual storms and
darkness at mid-day.

My home was on the other side of the city and the
Passover Sabbath would soon begin. My thoughts
were that, now he had gone, his followers, that
group of freed, joy-filled people I had so envied,
admired, scorned, hated, would lose heart and
disperse and threaten me no more. He was gone. The
Law had prevailed and I would re-apply myself to its
study and try again to live a life in obedience to it.
The sun was at the horizon's edge as I reached my
courtyard. I turned to marvel and there deep in the
sunset — was it vision or fantasy or a shocked

memory? — I saw again that blood-stained figure, embraced by, uplifted in the rays of the dying sun. I turned away and quickly entered the dim courtyard.

I hardly remember the formalities of that Passover evening. A few young students had joined me and the rituals had been carried out. I played my part meticulously, automatically, my mind and feelings far from the lighted candle, the familiar words, the child's traditional questioning and the traditional answers. At last I crossed the courtyard and withdrew to my room, cast off my robes and lay on my bed. Was I feverish? Ill? Why this strange, bewildered, uncoordinated thinking? A numb emptiness, my mind, my will, my heart in conflict? The only thing I could see clearly, try as I would to push it away, was that body crucified on that cross. I had seen dead bodies before. It was not death as horror or novelty that held me. It was the man. I had been jealous of him, jealous of his hold on Stephen, jealous of Stephen's love for him. Why then did I not feel a total sense of relief as I looked at him, lifeless, hanging there? — A beautiful, virile, healthy body, broken? He was crucified, dead and, probably, by now, flung in the pauper's grave. Why could I not dismiss him from my mind? Be eager to go back to Stephen and claim his love, as it had been for me before he came across the Galilean upstart?

I tossed and turned all that night and only now do I know that I was fighting against Love. That broken body kept appearing before me, hanging lifeless on that wooden scaffold — blood-stained against the sunset. Was I witnessing death or life? Both were one and were real. Men had done all they could to destroy that man and yet, beyond, above that death was life.

I beat the vision back, over and over, but it would not fade. I rejoiced at his death, for Stephen, by his lover's dying, was set free to give me the love I longed for. The Law had been upheld by both Pharisees and Sadducees and both had condemned Jesus to death. He had committed blasphemy, they said, defied the Law, ignored the traditions and was indifferent to Temple ritual and sacrifice. I could go along with most of them in that, for I was a scholarly Pharisee and tested all details of the Law against the light of reason as Gamaliel had always so surely taught. Yet there was a conflict for me far deeper than this. My faith was not only in the Law, neither was it solely in the Jewish faith, though I most deeply respected and reverenced the God of Abraham, Isaac, Jacob, Moses and the prophets. Without the knowledge of God revealed to me by my family and upbringing and later studies I would never have known the one true God, but only the multifarious hierarchy of Greek, Roman, Egyptian gods whose myths and mysteries had so often come my way and enthralled me in the Tarsus days. Yet, deepest of all in me was my faith in the love and respect of man for man. Throughout my life I had looked up to, admired, almost I would say, worshipped and adored the last and highest being created by God — Adam, the perfect man. I loved his physical strength and form as seen in games, athletics, all the graces of skill and movement. I remember the one and only chariot race I went to when I was about ten. The horses terrified and towered over me, but it was the charioteer who rivetted me! The leg muscles tensed to balance, the arms to wield flail and rein, the eyes flashing, jaw set and everything focussed for power and control, not merely of his own body, but his will controlling those foaming, racing animals before him. I was determined to grow to have such power and such strength, till I had no fear in me at all. Power and might and conquest would overcome all fear.

I loved man's mind as revealed by reason and logical thought and my studies of the Law and its intricate detail which, finally, Gamaliel made so vital for me. I loved man's creative, artistic, imaginative skills in sculpture, painting, architecture, drama; in wood, clay, stone, or in story-tale, myth or legend. When these skills emerged in cities and temples, theatres and statues I could only marvel and wonder and when I saw all this beauty gathered in physical form in those men, Stephen, Articus, Simeon, Tholemy, so many who had been my lovers, the abstractions of Law and the smell of Temple sacrifices and incense at any altar paled into pathetic impotence. Why did this conflict wrestle in me that night and why did that dead body, bloody, broken, destroyed, keep returning in the dark silence and haunt, even taunt, me? Perhaps I was more afraid of death than I had realised for there was no life there. No taunting. Only death.

I think, at last, I slept fitfully and then my old dream returned, so different from the recurring reality of that dead man. I was caught again in the battle to the death between Good and Evil. There were flashing beams of light but now they were streaked with blood breaking through the overwhelming darkness and I was tossed to and fro, unsure where Goodness lay and where Evil, and what was Truth. When dawn broke I awoke and knew I must go to Stephen for in the night I had shared his pain. It never crossed my mind that I was never to see him alive in the flesh again.

We move camp tomorrow. My friends have moved me to a small tent alone. "Friend." Naboth had said, "when we pack to move camp in the morning we do it in a very orderly way. All the men and women have their place. We take three days and are then ready, before dawn on the third day to move on. You are welcome to move with us but it would not be possible, as we know you would wish, to give you tasks in the preparation. If you would accept our hospitality in a small tent alongside until we travel you would be welcome."

I am content and grateful to accept this. In my days here I am renewing, repairing and replacing their floor-mats and hangings and they recognise this as fair payment for the hospitality they are giving me. What they are giving me cannot be repaid in service, for it is their unquestioning acceptance of me, as I am, that has been their greatest gift. I shall travel with them to their next camp which is to be south as far as the Yarmuk river. Then they will journey east towards Baghdad, trading spices, dried fruit and wine for cloth, gold, incense, ivory and pearls and then I must decide the way that I must go.

So it has happened as they said and I have had three peaceful days, oblivious of the noise of packing and storing outside and the shouts and cries and orders. I think over and over again of this miracle of revelation to me and the change in me. What has changed? I am still Saul, Pharisee, Doctor of the Law, follower of Moses; still Paul, the boy influenced by the stories and myths of the Greek tradition. I am Hebrew of the Hebrews and also a citizen of Rome. I am a human being with a man's needs, hungers, desires and a man hungering for the truth revealed to the wise of every age and to my own people, God's chosen ones. What then is the truth about myself? Who am I and for what purpose am I created?

Though I have written the above I know also that I am not these many people. I am one. My pen stays poised as I dwell long on my first question. What has changed? This, I think, is my answer. The great change that has changed me from the old Saul to the new Paul is that love has been given to me, specifically to me, unchangeably, through the generosity and graciousness of a man, so truly and completely human, so at one with his Creator that he has passed through death to life that is eternal and immortal. This man, Jesus, out of love for me, has called me. I, who hated him and loathed and persecuted all those he had called to him, am now one of them, beloved as they are. Whether Jew or Gentile, male or female, bond or free, wise or foolish, he loves us all and is alive with and in us and I love him because he first loved me. This is the way in which I now see myself and those around me. I see this Bedouin family, whom I have known for such a short time, in the light of the love of Jesus, the Christ.

I rose from my writing and went outside. I watched them all at the final work of striking camp. They were scouring pots, rolling mats, binding sticks and thorns, hauling sacks. I saw them through Love's eyes, each at heart in deep need of the joy I knew in being loved. Then I saw two men fighting, shouting at each other. One held a young ram by the horns, its body firmly gripped between his legs. The other attacked him, beat and pummelled him for possession of the ram. Finally, the ram broke free and galloped up the hillside and the men, one now with a knife drawn, fell on each other in fierce rage. I ran forward to separate them.

"Peace!" I shouted. "Peace!" and one yelled at me,

"Mind your own business, Rabbi! Your Law has no hold over us!" and one of them kicked out at me and shrugged me off where I clutched him.

Their cries brought other men to the scene and they were dragged apart and led off in different directions, shouting angrily and, no doubt, in some way the quarrel has now been resolved.

'Beloved of God!' I thought. Love made each of those men in Love's image, for the fulfilling of the purpose of creation. Why then the quarrelling and rage? And I remembered my own rage, my envy, my jealousy, my deep longing, though I had hardly known for what I hungered. Now I know. I had longed to be loved as I now know I am, without cause, without effort, not for what I might be but for what I am, a necessary part of Love's creation.

Two Days and a Sabbath Later

The sun is setting as I write. The tents are down and folded, each load on the ground beside a camel. The sheep and goats are close at hand and the boys and men will sleep near them so that they do not stray. One tent beside mine remains where the women and small children will sleep to-night. A last meal will be ready before day-break and then the camels will finally be loaded and we shall move off. We are to travel south towards the King's Highway and I shall travel with them and camp again somewhere near the Yarmuk river.

Before I sleep to-night I would use the last oil in my lamp to record the story Ananias told me of the last night of Jesus' earthly life when he and his closest friends kept the Passover meal together. Ananias had not been there but he had heard the story from James Bar Alpheus. Ananias told it to me, carefully, step by step, with his gentle, steady, sure reverence for the truth. It seems that for those who were there every act of Jesus was full of meaning; a personal parable for each of them so that they are retelling, with immense and loving care the new symbolism of each word and detail and event. Certainly, as Ananias told me, I moved with him through every detail of that night. This was that same man who, so short a time later, was to be the broken body I had seen on the cross. Now he is the man I love, the Light and Love that met me in my revelation wadi. For this reason I listened, rapt, as Ananias talked. For this reason I must record the events on that last night in that upper room where, I learnt, he and his followers had so often met before. When Ananias finished and left me I felt closer to my Lord than ever and the man from Nazareth, crucified and resurrected, was one with me. As I write I know these words carry a deeper meaning than I realise, even as I write them, and they will carry meaning through the years with profoundly mystical and spiritual power.

Jesus saw himself that night as embodying all the symbols of Passover tradition. He was the Pascal Lamb whose blood was to mark the way out of bondage to the freedom of life in Love. They all felt afterwards that he had known, as they could not, what lay ahead for him. He was the unleavened bread of sincerity and truth. He was the Passover candle, the Light of the Logos in the world; the true Light, which, as Greek mythology tells, lights the soul of every man born into the world.

As Ananias spoke I had been deeply moved, for in these symbols I recognised yet again that the old Law which had enslaved me was not destroyed but was a step for me on Life's ladder to the Love of my Beloved. "This is my blood," he had said as he passed the cup symbolising the blood of the lamb. "Drink this," he had said to them, "in remembrance" − no longer of Moses leading the children of Israel out of Egypt, but − "of me" − of his leading of us from the imprisonment of the Law into the freedom of Love. The old Law has been surpassed and fulfilled.

"This is my body," he had said, breaking the Passover loaf to share with them, and, so soon after, the body of that man, so full of sincerity and truth, was broken on the cross, uncomplaining, totally accepting, because he loved even those who demanded, ordered or executed his death. That mutilated body, that blood was shed by me, for I slew him as much as any Roman soldiers who drove in the nails, any Pharisee who cursed him, anyone in the mob who yelled for his crucifixion, I just happened not to be there. I had never met him. Yet the Law I taught slew him and I had been glad that he was dead.

Those thoughts tormented me until I fell asleep. I have slept fitfully and awakened early. Stars are still twinkling faintly and dawn is near. I listen to the silence as if the still hidden sun has alerted the very stones to hold their breath and in an awesome stillness wait for the Light that heralds a new day, With the world I hold my breath but my heart sings to Love, my God and Father, to praise Him for the gift to me of His son, my brother, my lover, Jesus, my Lord, Christ.

Soon the camp came to life and the final loading of the camels began, the folding of my small tent, the stacking of cooking pots and bedding, the sealing of oil and water and fire, till all were stowed firmly, safely, and as the sky turned to rose just before sunrise we were ready to move on. Since then, of course, I have had no time to write and have, indeed, been glad of the rest from writing and the chance to mix with and talk to the men and children as we journeyed. We were to sleep alongside the beasts on that first night. It was a bleak desert spot with little grazing for the sheep and goats but Naboth knew a wadi near, where there was a deep, sure trickle of water, so with much bleating and scattering of stones the flock was watered and finally settled for the night.

The women had made a vegetable stew. One large pot was heated over a thorn fire and when we had eaten we were glad to wrap our cloaks round us and huddle together close to the camels. Their snorts and mumbles and stench were not so familiar that I was able to close ears and nostrils as Naboth next to me could do. He was soon snoring peacefully. Between us young Reuben slept deeply, undisturbed by any sound or movement.

I lay half asleep thinking of words Ananias had told me − "I am in my Father and my Father in me." These were Jesus' words and Ananias and the disciples had pondered long over them in those days after the crucifixion when they felt him so close to them.

'Father,' Ananias had said, had been Jesus' form of addressing God and this was the secret of his relationship. His sonship. Our sonship. My concept of 'Father' had been based on fear and finally hatred of my human father but I could recognise that there is often a loving trust and mutual dependency between father and son. I watch it often here amongst these Bedouin people. Young Reuben had shared this trust with me, and as he and Naboth and I huddle close alongside the camel to-night I learn of a father's love. Reuben is experiencing already a father's love though this is only a human shadow of the Love of God for His children of which Jesus spoke when he said, "I am in the Father and the Father in me."

Journey to the Yarmuk River

The next morning we set off again. It did not take long to be away and by midday we had rounded the shoulder of Mount Hermon and dropped down by a rough track alongside the Raqqad river. Vegetation was becoming green and the track led through oak trees. The animals were slow to move, cropping any tasty shoot in their path and needing constant shouts from the children and shepherds to keep then moving. Finally the Raqqad joined the great Yarmuk river and we passed a hot spring strangely bubbling through the cold water. It was said to have healing properties and there was an old Greek sarcophagus by the water used as a trough to catch the cold water for drinking. As I bathed my hands I thought it was like my Lord's love for me, warm on my heart.

Local people were gathered there and I sat for a time listening to them. I was deliberately the listener, partly because their language was unfamiliar with many words and phrases different from the Aramaic of Jerusalem. I felt a man of two worlds — not merely the two worlds of Tarsus and Jerusalem nor the two worlds of Greek philosophy and Jewish Torah; with those worlds I am familiar, but now I am a citizen of earth and heaven, of body and spirit, through Jesus' love for me.

Sitting by that sarcophagus I listened to the talk of those around me and saw those people — rich merchants, beggars, strong young men and gracious women, shouting children, sleeping or crying babies in their mother's arms, coming to the water, vital for earthly life as Love was vital for the life of their spirits.

"Paul!" It was Naboth calling me. "Why so withdrawn to-day? Come and join us! We have met our cousins returning from the desert to Damascus." So I joined them and the cousins were willing to deliver a message from me to Judas in Straight Street to tell the brethren where I was and that I was still this side of Jordan having delayed my return to Jerusalem.

Soon we left the crowds by the river and climbed again, skirting the town of Abila and reached the top of a mountain ridge, on a curving plateau, looking down into the river valley below. In the misty distance was Tiberias where so much of my Lord's life had been lived; unknown country to me. Below were narrow clefts and ravines where several small streams fell down to the Yarmuk. It was very beautiful. "Here we will camp," said Naboth. The message went round and the unloading and pitching of tents began. "We will probably stay here, Paul, for several weeks," he told me. They would sow small patches of barley, wheat and corn and stay until it was harvested, journeying daily to Abila, one of the ten cities of the Decapolis region or to the villages and markets round, to buy merchandise and fruit to dry, figs, apricots and plums to trade beyond Dera and on the road to Baghdad.

"May I stay with you a little longer?" I asked and Naboth welcomed me to stay as long as I wished and young Reuben clutched my sleeve to show his acceptance of me. I will stay with them until I know my Lord is calling me, perhaps to Jerusalem, or at least over Jordan, as the first step of my journey towards the Gentile world where I am coming to feel my life is to be spent. Perhaps I will stay in the camp long enough to complete the writing of this journal. By then I hope my Lord will have made clear to me the truth behind the great perplexities and stumbling blocks that for so long have blinded and bound me and inhibited my freedom to love.

For these first few days in our new encampment I have been mixing with them all. I am looking for commissions by which I can use my skills for them as they so graciously give theirs to me. Fortunately my skill as a weaver is very acceptable and I have specialised in the heavy goat-hair cloth in black and brown which is needed for the tents, so there is much I am able to do for them in repairs and replacements. This has brought me often into contact with the women. They are as shy with me as I am with them. They have not often come close to a Doctor of the Law from Jerusalem, or a young man from far off Tarsus who knows Antioch and Sidon and speaks four languages! I wondered what stories they had heard of me from around Damascus? Had they heard of my savage persecutions or had they heard of me as an untrustworthy turn-coat or spy? It was well known that news from far and wide and not just local tittle-tattle was spread through the women's tents. The secrets men shared with their women at night all too often made the gossip of the women at the well and became the tales round the cooking fires and grindstones or while washing clothes in the river. I am easily shy of them too, having never had a chance to be close to women, in my family or elsewhere. I have been almost exclusively in a man's world all my life.

Soon I found enough work to fill my days and there is time also to withdraw into the woods or down by one of the rivers or into my tent when the day's work is finished. The daily round has become familiar and I have relaxed into its pattern and again prepared parchment for writing. I know most of the people — there are about forty of us in the camp at this time — and I am finding it daily easier to see each one through the eyes of Love and marvel at each one's uniqueness and gifts. I find that I had, before my resurrection wadi experience, selected and rejected ruthlessly those whom I liked and disliked. I had thought my likings showed discrimination and my likings were my loves for they satisfied my hungers and desires and fed my pride. My dislikes — of the dull or deformed or diseased — were because my rejection of them had been approved by others and they were seen by most people to be unlovable and to be punished for their sins. How Christ in me transforms that view. The Christ is in each of them. God loves every creature He has made, each one unique and each shining with a light of individual brightness. How have I been unable to see? Oh, there are the world's rogues and rascals about, lawbreakers and thieves and the power-ridden and self-righteous. I had been one of them. But only mortal eyes label them in that way. Jesus on earth had loved them all. They were all his brothers, begotten of the same Father, light from Light. But they, as I, had never known this and we all struggled to out-do the other man, conquer the Law, climb to heaven by our own phylacteries and fringes. Would it ever be habitual for me to recognise all people as children of God and heirs of His Kingdom?

Two months ago I had a dream. Reality, dream and vision are hard to separate. All are experiences through which we can reach the truth of Love. Stephen came to me clearly and vividly. He is always in my thoughts and in my heart but never have I 'seen' him to 'converse' with him as I did that night. One minute he was streaming with blood as I had last seen him when they were stoning him. The next minute I saw him as he was that day when we first met − young, virile, and beautiful, leaning against the Temple pillar in Tarsus not long before he sailed to Antioch on his way to Jerusalem. Then, in my dream, he came close and stood over me and I raised myself on my elbow to see him more clearly, aware and yet unbelieving.

"Paul," he said, "I know now that you know him as I know him. Jesus claimed me as his in Jerusalem, as he claimed you on your way to Damascus. I know, as you do, that he loves us, not with human love but with the Love that is God. He knew himself beloved of God and we, his brothers, beloved also. He loved us before we loved him and when I realised this, I realised that our search, that search that you and I knew so well, was not that we might make love but that we might be loved as fervently as we loved ourselves. That was our longing. It was recognition of our own worth we sought and he loved me for what I was and as I was. No greater gift could have been given me. I was his slave for ever when I saw God's Love for me through his eyes; not a slave in serfdom but a free slave, choosing him as my Master for ever. I serve him now as faithfully as I did in those last weeks before his crucifixion and before my death and as I will for evermore, and as you will, Paul."

There was silence between us. Then came a peace that the world cannot give. I had not visited Stephen again after I visited him on the day of Jesus' death. I had been too hurt, too angry, to go back and when rumours reached me saying that the man, Jesus, had never died, that an imposter was crucified instead, that his body had been stolen when he had been taken down from the cross and was restored to life, it was intolerable. I knew the man was dead. I had seen him. What could I have said to Stephen if I had gone to him? I was a Pharisee. I believed that the soul lived on after the death of the body but the nature of the life that lay ahead was hidden in the shades of Sheol. What use was an argument with one who seemed so clearly to have been brain-washed and caught in a collective emotional substitute for an unbearable grief? But in the silence between us two nights ago, in my dream, there was a peace and a joy in our closeness, different from any sharing we had known before.

At last I said, "Stephen, I was there when you died." (On the other side of death does he already know? I wondered.) I realised that we were together in the spirit and that I was closer to him than had ever been humanly possible. "I could not let you know how bitterly jealous I was of you," I confessed to him, "as I was of all those Galilean friends who perpetually hung around Jesus and I was envious of your freedom. You were all so free and fearless and you, yourself, were so different when, once or twice I had seen you with them. You were free and guiltless, while I was bound by the Law, always failing, for all my struggles and studies. I watched you early on the morning of the day you died. You were in the Court of the Gentiles with two small boys who seemed to be hanging on your every word. Suddenly, they ran off and you called after them, 'Come tomorrow at this time and I will tell you more about him and you will meet him, too.' I was deeply shocked Stephen, for I knew that you spoke of Jesus and, for the first time, I knew of falsehood in you for I had seen the man hanging there, undeniably dead.

"When I left after my last visit to you, Stephen," I told him in my dream, "I walked home outside the city wall and by chance I saw him hanging dead on the cross. There was no doubt, yet you, you of all people, whom I trusted so deeply, were one of those spreading the pathetic rumours that he was alive. While you believed that, it was useless for me to think that I could ever win back your love for me. I was wretched and deeply hurt and consumed by jealousy of what Jesus had meant to you, even though he was then dead and could only be, for ever, no more than a memory. 'Not even his death can stop them,' I had thought. During the next days I spoke often to the scribes and elders about the rumours and I had told them I would willingly take on the responsibility of stamping out the gossip and those responsible for it. If it had just remained with the women where, apparently, much of it had begun, there would have been little need for alarm. Women have little else to fill their lives but gossip and theirs soon goes underground and gets forgotten. But the men — this was more dangerous and your name came up from time to time to fan my jealousy and despair.

"Then came that day, Stephen, when in a noisy frenzy I found myself mixed up with a crowd moving from the Outer Court of the Council chamber. They were mostly, I thought, from the freedmen synagogue, some from Asia and Alexandria from their accent, but there were Council members there too and lawyers and then I saw — you know what I saw, Stephen. You were in the middle of the crowd and they were shouting for your death. I heard what you said in answer to their questions and I was horrified. It seemed to me that you flaunted and twisted our history, our traditions, our leaders — you, who had hung on my every word in those days when we studied the Law together. I recognised the pattern of Gamaliel's lecture notes which I had lent you and you used them to make your points. Then, as I looked, straining to see over the crowd, for, arriving late, I was at the back, I saw you through the eyes of human love, as I had done so many times before and you were young and strong and beautiful and looked like an angel. I was carried away with longing for your love and never heard the last part of your speech until suddenly I saw you transfigured and you looked up and called out and your words were drowned by the shouts and clamouring and you were driven out of the Council chamber and I followed. I stood at the back by a pile of cloaks they had flung down and then the hail of stones began and your face and body streamed with blood and you fell. I wept, with love for you and my love was mixed with rage and jealousy and hatred and, Stephen, I heard your last cry. Your last words rang out and — why did such fury fill me?"

I paused. "You had not met Jesus then," Stephen said gently and I woke, with tears streaming down my face and I lay in the darkness, confused and unhappy. Little by little my tears for the man I had been at Stephen's stoning died away. I was dearly loved. Christ in me rose again and I knew in me the love and spirit of my Lord. Jesus had appeared to me at the resurrection wadi. He saw me as my Creator saw me, made in His image. He loves the truth about me and accepts me as I am. All I have ever been is accepted, loved, and will never fade or die.

That 'dream' − yet it was no dream − is now several days ago. Whether Stephen was well aware before I spoke of all I told him, whether those who have died remember all the details of their lives on earth and know the experiences of those who live on after they have gone, I cannot know. I only know that our sharing together of the Love we now know through the Lord Jesus meant that, in that 'dream' we knew a closeness and peace and shared a Love past mortal understanding. Jesus, through his living and dying and rising again, in unswerving awareness that he was a unique son of his Father, God, and his seeing each of us as similarly beloved, had drawn Stephen and me together in a profoundly loving brotherhood as could have been shown to us in no other way. So, marvelling at the mystery and reality of it all, in experience, I went on my way through the days − until yesterday.

Timothy

Yesterday brought about a strangely unexpected and distressing episode. If I am to be true to myself I must look closely at it and write of it for I am tempted to pretend it could never happen.

I went out in the early morning with the men for we were packed up and ready to move on again. A storm of heavy rain had fallen ten days before in a valley three hours' journey from our camp and as our grazing was becoming sparse it was decided that the sheep and goats should be driven over there for some days for the fresh growth that would follow the rains. I decided to go with them. I could help to drive the animals and it was difficult for me to find enough to do in the camp to repay their hospitality. I had a small bivouac tent I had made for just such an occasion, light and easy on my back.

The sheep and goats were soon being driven ahead by the shepherd boys. There was a young boy standing leaning on a staff at the back of the flocks. He was not one who had come to my attention before though I knew him by sight. He did not seem to be pure Bedouin. He turned and our eyes met. I turned away and then turned my eyes back again. Again our eyes met and we held each other in a fearless gaze and I knew what was happening for I felt the fire in my loins, the flaming in my blood, the sweat, all the signs of physical desire I had known so often and so well. I knew he knew it too. Someone called him as the animals were straying and his job was to keep them moving, so he ran up the slope to gather them back. His tunic flew wide and his arms were raised as he waved his staff and the sheep and goats ran bleating into the rest of the herd. The hillside with its cropped clumps of thorn and its sandy gravel was still and the rolling desert held its breath as I turned back to drive the animals and try to forget.

We camped soon after noon in a small wadi with shady trees, oleander and running water and later, after dark, standing right at the back with firelight glinting in the shadow, he was there again. Again our eyes met and we could not let each other go. Many times I turned away and then turned back again and our eyes spoke and I knew what we were saying. My Lord was forgotten. Christ in me was forgotten. Stephen was far from me. I was caught totally in the desires and hungers of mortal flesh and wanted that boy close to me, young, strong, hot and full of life-giving energy which we knew, as our eyes met, we could share together.

Two more days have passed during which I have seen him only distantly. I try to forget him. I love him humanly and cannot still the passion and hunger in me for his love. I tossed restlessly to and fro with desire for him and the deep sleep and peace I had known in the arms of my Lord had gone. The stars shone and a waning moon rose slowly and set. Every muffled bleat of a lamb or sharp bark of a desert fox or jackal alerted me again to my sleepless hunger.

Then, last night, the sixth night after our recognition of our mutual longing, I saw my tent cover drawn back a little further and then a gentle pressure fell on my blanket. A groping hand caught my ankle and I gasped. I knew he had come. His hand reached up to my knee and I reached down to draw him gently closer. I was on fire for him as he was for me. We held our breath in silence for a moment under the timeless sky and I watched through the tent door where a star watched us, twinkling, watching, twinkling, waiting, ceaselessly revealing the handiwork and mystery of creation. I broke out in sweat and then, in gulping tears, pulled the boy close. He tried to twist and fumble but I held him firmly with a wrestler's grip.

Then I heard Stephen's voice. "Look," he said, "I see the heavens open and the Son of Man standing at the right hand of God." In the deep blue night sky, with that clear star sparkling, Stephen was with me and his spirit, the Christos, was in that tent. Then I knew again my true lover and Lord and it was he who held me close as I held the boy. I saw again that body on the cross and knew the mortal struggle was over. I relaxed my wrestler's grip and drew the boy to me. Neither he nor I now moved. Then gently I pushed him away from me. I felt him, unresisting, move to the end of the blanket. His weight had gone. The tent flap was drawn a little and fell. I heard no footfall but only the singing silence of the night and the sky was now full of a myriad stars. Had he been or had it been a dream?

It had been no dream. As the first light of a new day broke, fear and horror and shame were with me. At first I thought my treachery and faithlessness to Love had thrown me into the hell of which our scriptures and the Law so surely spoke. The 'jealous God' and 'Thou shalt have none other gods'. Fear. Horror. Shame. For I, who have known a greater

Love, have yearned for a lesser. How can I ever make amends? Is my yearning for the closeness of a fellow human being, that yearning in which every part of the physical man that I am is caught, is that the enemy, the opposite, of the Love in which my life has lately been lived? If that is true I know a war in my members that means I am on a battleground for ever. I, wretched man that I feel myself to be, have descended lower than Hades, to a hell deeper than any spoken of in ancient myth or Jewish Law.

We returned to the encampment the day after I wrote the above. In the days since then I have not seen the boy at all. I have kept alone and am slowly, surely, coming to understand and interpret the experiences of these days and of these things I must now try to write.

The marvel and joy of Love as shown in Jesus is that it is freely given and never withdrawn. If I write this over and over in this journal it is because I am struggling to get used to it, accept it, believe in it and never take it for granted, whatever experiences come my way to shake my faith. It is so new and so entirely different from the God of Whom I learnt in the Law. God, Who gave the Law, forever sits in judgement. 'Thou, God, seest me' can be a frightening thought, for we all know deep within us how great is our love of self, how deep our hunger to be loved and how fear-filled and small is our love for others. Yet how could we know its smallness if we were not aware, deep within us, of the heights and depths of Love? From whence did that knowledge come?

Always I knew and, indeed, since a child, the Law had taught me that I must love the Lord my God with heart, mind, soul and strength and that less

than this was failure, sin, incurring God's wrath,
judgement, punishment. I would never have known
sin if I had not studied the Law. Now, I rejoice in
saying, "Thou, God, seest me", for He sees me in
love. It is liberating, to know that I am seen, known,
understood, made as I am, in His image, loved, now,
to-day, not in a distant tomorrow if I work, strive
and struggle to be worthy. This is my new unshake-
able faith — I am beloved by the love seen in my
risen Lord, Jesus. But how do I reconcile this with
my love for the shepherd boy for whose love I
hungered?

I realise now that Stephen came to me in that
dream, in the days preceding my encounter with the
young Bedouin, by the direct will of God, to keep me
alert and aware of the highest and so prepare me for
the experience that lay ahead. Stephen and I had
shared our experience of Love through the Lord
Jesus and Stephen's appearing to me was a preparation of my thought and feeling for meeting that boy.
My love for him, yes, a mortal, sexual love, was
neither to be judged right nor wrong. We were
struggling to express the highest loving we could
then share in our encounter together. Stephen and I
had first known a similar love together and because
each of us was, later, to be given a deeper love by our
Lord Jesus and through him for each other, so we
have climbed to heights and depths of loving, giving
and receiving, unknown before. Our mortal bodies
are in subjection to our liberated spirits and we have
moved from mortal man's feelings to a realm of
awareness of Love that casts out all fear and
torment. The shepherd boy knew it. He has since
told me that when he slipped away from me that
night to go to his place near the sheep, after initial

frustration and disappointment a strange joy made him long to shout aloud. Each of us, deep within, knew ourselves loved of a Love deeper than any feeling we had for each other.

We speak to each other often now. We meet when we can and he is fascinated and awed as I tell him my story and about Jesus, my Lord. Could he have found Love through me as I first found It in Jesus? The Spirit of God dwelling in each of us? 'Deep calling unto deep?' Is this the 'Christ' in us reaching out in love to one another? The Saviour for whom Judaism longs, found first in Jesus and through him, relayed by love to each other? Is Messiah, first, an individual in Jesus, then to become a loving fellowship of all mankind sharing his loving spirit? This is a strange unfolding mystery. We are all unfolding from glory to glory. That glory, first seen in Jesus, is as we too are seen and known through the eyes and mind of our Father, Creator, Who loves us, not as we appear but as we truly are. Is this the secret of Jesus' love? Is this the Spirit of Messiah now in the world and is this the truth I am called to spread?

From Child to Scholar

I have had little time in the last days to write my journal. It has been lambing time. I never thought that I, Gamaliel's top scholar, Rabbi of Jerusalem, would find myself on the hillsides of Abila, in Decapolis, beyond Jordan, holding and soothing an anxious ewe struggling to give birth. I must admit to holding the head end, not having any skill to be of help elsewhere, for I am a man of town and city and this has been a new experience for me. How often I have said, read and chanted the psalms of David, but always now, the hills of Decapolis will be in my mind when I sing the Shepherd King's psalms.

The child, the boy, the young man I have been and the life that has been mine, with all its opportunities, perplexities, strugglings, restraints and mistakes, I believe was known, expected and understood by my Maker before my earthly days began. Love has given me life. Love has made me in His image. I feel I am brought to a new birth as much as any of these young lambs coming to birth around us. Love has revealed Himself to me step by step, and finally through my Lord Jesus' love for me. There have been no mistakes. Every moment is a gift to me for my learning of Love because I am beloved. Today, on the hills above Abila I am as I am. I look backwards to my birth on earth and press forward to my earthly death, living only in this moment, for now is Love giving me life.

I must try to look back objectively to the Tarsus years from my birth to later adolescence for I am seeing, increasingly clearly, a pattern emerging. My growth and upbringing and my own attitude and response I realise now was predestined and acceptable to God, my Creator. From the moment of my conception, and in every moment of time since then, I have been in His hands, shaped, understood and beloved, even in those nights and days seen as sinful in the eyes of the Law.

When I look back on my first days in Jerusalem I realise that it was hard for a young man such as I was to live without problems in a university city centred on the Temple. Jerusalem seethed with cosmopolitan life; so many languages were spoken; the people were under direct rule from Rome, however much was delegated to the King or permitted to the Temple authorities. We were subjected ruthlessly on all sides to the laws and traditions of our religion and to the laws and taxes of our conquerors and all these at a seat of learning famed throughout the world, second only to Alexandria. It was far stricter and more restrictive than the free and easy life I had known even in a strictly Jewish family such as ours in Tarsus. I quickly realised that it was because of the rigorous disciplines under which I would live that my father had sent me to study law in Jerusalem under Gamaliel.

In many ways I was like my father. This was part of my problem. I was the fifth child and the first-born son, and my mother died in giving me birth. Only one other child had survived, the first-born, Miriam, fourteen years older than I. In theory she was old enough to take the place of my mother but she was betrothed just before my birth and felt the loss of her mother deeply. She never showed much feeling and certainly no warmth towards me, and I can remember her saying when, as a small boy, she scolded me for breaking a water pot, "You were always clumsy. You even killed our mother with your clumsiness when you were born." Unforgettable and horrifying words. Though I was young I was aware of her deep resentment of me. I was told by one of my uncles that when my mother became pregnant for the fifth time — after a miscarriage and then two daughters who each died in infancy — my father had given up hope of a son and had no enthusiasm for the birth of yet another daughter. He had taken care to be away from home when I was born and then, when my mother died and they sent for him, he returned to find his son, puny and sick and he spent hours in the synagogue praying and making sacrifices for my survival. His prayers were answered through the devoted care of my grandmother and the reluctant, casual attention of my sister.

My father ran a business exporting rugs, carpets and tent hangings and had been made a Roman citizen some years before my birth because of his service to the export trade of the city. He seemed to be so little at home and, because I had no mother, I grew up much on my own, easily making friends with whoever I chose, down by the port, in the market or up amongst the rocks and caves in the mountains behind Tarsus. I have inherited from my father his stubborn independence, strong will, boundless energy, acute intelligence and hasty temper.

As I grew to adolescence, problems arose that puzzled me. My friends and I shared experiences of growing bodies and wild emotions gleaned from the older youths whom we admired and courted. We experienced physical delights undreamt of. I joined wild gangs and groups and would escape, usually in the early evening after school and extra studies, for adventures and exploits that, had my father known, would have resulted in severe punishment. According to the law I deserved death! When he was at home he ruled me with a rod of iron, recognising, I think, and fearing, much of his character in me. I reacted to his reproofs by being sullen and morose and grew further and further from any concern or interest in parent, family or home. This was incomprehensible to my father as it would have been to any traditional Jew.

My life, from childhood, through adolescence, became a private revolt against father, family and Law. Secretly I worshipped the statues of the Greek gods; I hero-worshipped Sapporis as we wrestled together; I loved Anthony and Gaius and many soldiers in the garrison, and knew, even after I was sent to Jerusalem, the burden and delight of many guilty secrets. The Torah imprisoned and shackled me. Now I am free. My bonds are broken, and I can look back with detachment and approve and understand that young man that I was.

What was it really that bound me? Was it my reluctant striving to be what my father wanted, that tied me? My father gave me the Law and I could never keep it. It tried to bend me to its way, and held me in iron bands of guilt and failure. It told me truths, about God, about my people and about myself but they were imposed upon me and never rang true in my heart or experience, though logically acceptable to my mind. I was led by a way that was hard and conforming and dull and restricting, and my soul cried out in pain as a quail caught in the hunter's snare. I longed to love and be loved and the ways in which I learnt of it were forbidden. 'Love God and your neighbour as yourself.' What love was that? How could I love a God who bound me by laws and precepts and threatened me with dire punishment and death when their fulfilment was beyond my strength or will? How could I love the neighbour who used me and exploited me when I gave him my love and who never loved me in return? How could I love myself? A son so despised by his father? Love must be greater than these.

Now I know that all these things that I thought to have been sins against God and man and myself are known, accepted and understood by Jesus, my lover. When they killed him they killed only the mortal in him and his resurrection brings life to my spirit. He is the Christ and I worship and love him. In him the Law is more than fulfilled; it is surpassed. I have seen him and know him and he is alive for evermore in me and through me. Here is the union in Love that I have struggled all through my life to find in my fellows. I am now a man, thirty years old, loved by and in love with Love itself. He is the beginning and end of all hungers, all searching, all struggles. Love is the supreme goal and God, of Greeks, Romans, Jews, barbarians, bond and free, rich and poor, far clearer, higher, surer than the truths veiled in the myths of Zeus, Athena, Pan or Artemis, beyond Osiris and the Babylonian stories of death and resurrection, closer than breathing. My lover, my Lord, and I at one with Christ in him.

I write and write here and words are hard and confining and my mind teems. Little Reuben last night was singing to his brother's lute, of the moon and the stars and the camp was stilled as he sang, for his childish voice was strong and true and he touched our feelings and our faith. Deep within us we know we are one with each other, with the universe, with our Maker. We are His and the moon and stars are His also. His Love for us is as a seed sown at birth in the heart of each one of us, uniting us with Him and with each other. We know it, and Jesus, my lover, lived it. The Law is in the learning, Love is in the living, and all my stirrings and growth towards Love, through childhood, youth and adolescence have been directing me to these heights.

Now my search is ended. What was it that I was seeking? I sought and have now found the lover who meets all my needs and I meet his. Who is he in whom I have found this freedom to love to the uttermost? He is a man whose earthly life had the freedom and courage that I longed for. He was never directed by Law or ordinance, but always knew, first and foremost, that he was beloved, a unique son of Love, who saw all those round him as beloved and unique, all fathered by Love. In seeing each one of us, whole and unclouded, he reverenced us, recognised us, loved us, gave himself to us and took from us all that we would give. I was surrounded by stories of things he did, people he met, healed, chose, loved. I had hated him. I saw fulfilled in him all that in me had been crushed, tied, bound by the life I lived. I hated him for being unscathed and free. I hated his followers, many of them crude Galilean fishermen, speaking a rough dialect; many women of the streets; money-grubbing tax-collectors and leprous drop-outs, while I, daily, hourly, struggled to be loved. Unable to give it, unable to receive it. Longing. Yet it never entered my head that he might have wanted me. I could have hunted him out, hung on the edge of the crowds, watched him, scorned him as so many rabbis did. I never thought of it. I went about my own business in my Pharisees' robes, with lawyers, scholars, priests as my companions. It was when Stephen, a fellow-student, got caught up in it, that it became more than I could bear. Stephen had been my lover, beautifully, happily and yet, because of our learning of the Law, it was also in a guilty, half-hearted way, and then I found I had lost him to the Galilean. I went to see Stephen one evening and, when I found him, all guilt had gone from him. He was laughing, bright-eyed and far beyond my reach. I touched him and he eagerly accepted my touch, but there was no hunger, no longing, no veiled lust in the touch returned. He was free, loved, fulfilled. I could not hate him, but I hated, with bitter jealousy, the man who had taken him from me.

I began to garner every scrap of news of the man Jesus, in the Temple, the streets and markets and my mind wrestled with plots and schemes for destroying him. Some said he was a Zealot, some said an Essene, some a harmless itinerant preacher from the country. Most people said it was all a passing thing and would soon die. Much later, after his death, a Roman centurion friend who had been on guard at the crosses when he died said, "You should have seen the fool. Blood ran down his face from a wreath they had shoved on his head for a joke, because he'd been called a King by the crowds.

His body writhed in pain and sweat poured off him. I jammed a spear in his side to finish him off." He had gone on, "A soldier must do his job, though I'm not a blood-thirsty man. His head fell forward and his body slumped and that was that — till next time. I don't often remember these criminals. Too many pass through my hands but there was a dignity about his death. He was more than a man."

I had been stunned by what he had said. I puzzled, wrestled, suffered, in jealousy and loneliness and anger, until after his death and after Stephen's death I heard his voice say, "Saul, Saul, why are you persecuting me?" And he was there, moving to me, ringed with blinding light, alive, giving me love, seeing me, as I saw him, in the light of Love.

It was the Love that I had always longed and hungered to receive. All my own loving had been that I might receive. Already I can look back on the young man I was, aware of the good and true and beautiful in himself, longing to be united with the good and true and beautiful in another. I had seen that supple, stripped, bronzed young athlete, that rugged muscular soldier, that young Jewish student, the curly-headed boy selling sparrows in the suk — I had seen myself in them all and as the child in me became man so my sexual physical hungers longed for fulfilment in union with my loves. This was all I knew of love — admiration, wonder and above all, my own longing, to be truly loved, truly close to, united with, love itself, wherever I could recognise it.

Then, in that blinding light when he came to me I saw, in a flash, this new Truth. I was beloved. All my earthly father had despised in me, all my desires and hungers and lusts that had driven me on that endless desperate search for the Ideal Lover were now gathered up and my desires were blessed, hallowed, by that crucified man over whom death had no power. I knew him to be alive and in love with me for evermore in time and in eternity.

I struggle to find words for these new feelings and ideas. I feel new-born into a world where I am stranger, where I must learn again to walk and talk. It is not easy here, with this busy world of the camp around me, but I snatch moments when I can and often write far into the night. I have bought a lamp and oil of my own for oil is expensive and I would not want my generous host to feel I was an extravagence to them.

This Jesus, my lover, is the Christ, the long-awaited Saviour, Messiah. We do not have to wait for some far-distant Judgement Day, for forgiveness of our wrongs, for the Christ to come. He is here. His Spirit flaming on the road to Damascus is in me. The Christ, the Messiah, sent from God to save the world is Christ Messiah in me. The light that illuminated my life then is in every child of God, and the world must know that, bond or free, Jew or Gentile, male or female, the eternal Spirit of Love is in us all. The Christ in each of us is called to demonstrate this Love in life, till the world is over-ruled and revealed as one.

I now know Love's Way, and the life that is chosen for me. Until a year ago I had thought I was struggling towards heaven by my good works, my efforts to study, learn and obey the Law. All else I believed led to the wrath and judgement of God for disobedience. I saw my role as a fighter for God's Law against any blasphemy and my persecution of the followers of Jesus was my God-given duty as I struggled to be a faithful Pharisee and an honoured rabbi. It is hard to believe I could have been so self-deceptive, so blind, to what I now see so clearly. Self-love and self-hate were at war in me and I had no idea where I was going. Now, one thing I know, where I was blind now I see. This love far surpasses any natural, earthly love that I know. I am on a new Way and now lead a new life in the Spirit of my Lord. As Jesus' body died on the cross, so I die with him and now I live with him in a new existence even under the conditions of this human life. That is why his body on the cross is for ever vividly before me. I am conformed to that image, and, as such, I am also a son of God, an heir, a co-heir with Jesus. I once lived faithful to my image of an earthly man; now I will be faithful to the image of the heavenly and my world is transformed in this new light. I no longer play on the earth's stage the role of Adam, the natural man, but the role of Christ, the spiritual man. The natural man in me must be for ever subservient to the spirit. No longer am I, Narcissus, in love with his reflected image but I live in love with a greater Self, the resurrected Jesus of the Damascus road. I am now free, freed from death and sin and alive only to Love in him. So I am beginning to see the Way he would have me go – into his world to give faith and hope and love to His children, all His beloved sons, my brothers.

I was called at this point into the men's tent for food. They had returned with the herds, had hobbled the male camel and tethered the rams and the men were already seated round the dish when I entered. They had spread a rug for me and gave me a goat skin of warm milk and fresh bread from the fire. Reuben came in. He had sung to his brother's lute last night and then sat with me under the stars with the other young people and I had told them of Moses and how God had called him, though he was so reluctant, to lead His people. Reuben came with a small lamb across his shoulders and sat close by me, cuddling closer with his lamb. I shared my bread and dates with him until his mother called him to fetch water. He was too young, I felt, to know directly about my Lord but not too young to know of our Father's Love and of himself as God's specially beloved son, for no one is too young to love and be loved and his brown eyes had sparkled last night when I had spoken of God as Father.

The new miracle of understanding that is becoming daily clearer to me is my Lord's acceptance of me as I am. I need no longer struggle to be different, to stifle or be untrue to my real self nor to push it behind me, too proud to acknowledge where I am ashamed.

Each thought held in the light of Love, each part of myself given in love is known and accepted. This is part of the great discovery. Jesus' words still and for ever will ring in my ears, "It is hard for you to kick against the goad." All my life I have kicked against the goad — that sharp point with which the farmer directs and pushes the ox along the furrow; that goad by which the rider spurs on the camel or the shepherd forces his reluctant sheep into the fold. It is used on the animal a man owns and trains, but man is no animal but spirit, made in God's image, incarnate. All along there has been a part of me that has kicked against being treated as animal. First I kicked against my father and his authority and teaching; then against Judaism, its culture and social patterning. Later, I kicked against the demands of the Law and the ridiculous conformity to pointless tradition and meaningless ritual. Finally, this kicking was against the Jesus Way, a fiercer outburst of malice and hate than I had ever known.

I can remember endless instances of my father's goads in wrath and anger. There was the final crisis when Uncle Ben Hadad had seen me at the baths, stripped and wrestling naked with the Roman boys and my father had questioned me and I had denied it all. Then Uncle Ben Hadad had produced my undergarment and I had to admit the truth. (I had thought when it was missing that the boys had hidden it in fun!) It was because of that final defiance that my father had sent me to Jerusalem. I knew then that never again could I be at home or at peace in my father's house and I would kick against that goad no longer. He had perhaps loved me in his own way but he tried to make me in his image rather than see me as the child of Love I really was. He had indeed owned and trained me as if I had been an animal, to be goaded into obedience. Now I know a Father's Love as seen by Jesus, I will strive willingly to obey. My father had tried to discipline me and teach me obedience. Then Uncle Ben Hadad's final proof of my waywardness was the final proof of his failure to make me fit to be his son and a son of the tribe of Benjamin. Neither the synagogue nor he himself were firm enough teachers and somehow the Law must be applied more surely. Only in Jerusalem and under Gamaliel's watchful eye could I be tamed.

It was sad that he knew nothing of the Christ in

me as I now know. All learning delighted me for I
had a scholarly mind. As a child I had learnt by
heart, not just the Law as I was made to, but, by
choice, all the psalms of David which I loved. I learnt
and loved, too, the stories of the patriarchs and all
the history of captivity and release, of prophets
pronouncing doom and our stubborn refusal to heed
their warnings. How I loved to learn, too, from the
Greek scholars and teachers in the gymnasium at
Tarsus, I learnt of the heroes of the Trojan war, of
Odysseus' journeyings, of the gods of Olympus, great
Zeus and Athena, of Artemis and Pan, of their
temples and altars and oracles and I had heard
Greek poetry and epic and tragedy. Mysteriously,
deep in my spirit, I knew all to be part of one Truth
and one with the self I knew myself to be. There was
one God over all, above and in all. I had fantasies of
my own omnipotence. My family were unaware that
I had made libations many times to the gods in the
Roman homes and on the altars of the Tarsus
theatre. To strict Jews this was a blasphemy and
heresy that was intolerable. I knew it, and buried
the thought deep within me, but never cast it out. I
had once planned to run away from home with some
young slave boys to Ephesus to offer a libation to the
Goddess Diana there. She was said to have great
power. I had been given a tiny little silver replica of
her, stolen by one of my young friends from his
master. I had lost it and was terrified it would be
found at home somewhere and my secret would be
discovered. I lived always with guilt and fear, for all
that I faced life with bravado. I longed for one final
libation that would be enough to atone for all my
non-conforming behaviour, for it was too much
part of me to give it up and live what would seem to

me to be a parody of my true self.

I studied astronomy and mathematics with delight. But it was those who taught me that I loved most, whether tutors in the Greek schools or my fellow students from whom I also learnt. I was easily infatuated by the beauty of an athlete, the skills of the gymnasium, the lines and forms of male beauty in the baths. This freedom from law and conformity bewitched me and I felt my body aglow with life and energy when I was in that world. Love of the ideal man was surely what we all longed for?

At home I stifled my hatred of conformity, and when it was deep buried I applied myself to the demands of my proud, strictly Benjamite family, directed and dominated by my father. I was fascinated by the Law's detailed complexity which stretched and stimulated my mind. My respect for it I kept from my father. It was perfectly possible to respond coldly, factually, to all his questioning and he was forced to recognise me as a capable, highly intelligent scholar. I think I even convinced him that I was without feeling and that my love for my fellow man, for the human marvel in the image of God that I worshipped in Greek temple or Roman bath, was out-grown. I had put away childish things. Generally speaking, it was easy to appear to obey the Law. Deep down my feelings scoffed at the ease with which I could 'fulfil' it! Then I had to − and this was less easy − 'fulfil' the minutiae. This was very much a matter of remembering trivial items of behaviour outside the Law. Then, the 'traditions', another vast body of behavioural demands. These, too, when I applied myself, could be fairly well remembered and fulfilled and my father's endless questioning and his watching of my every move could, rather to his annoyance, I feel, be reasonably satisfied. He never lost his suspicion of me and goaded me mercilessly. Was he afraid of himself in me? Himself he could handle, but his wilful son was a greater problem.

While this study, this endless watching and cross-examination was on, it was hard for me to escape to my friends at the barracks, or the baths or the agora. The synagogue congregation was too large for me easily to be free. If I did find the chance for a word with Silvanus or Stephen's brother, there was little chance for more than their chiding me for my two-facedness or laughter at my Jewish dress and outward conformity. Then came the day of my fool-hardy escape to the baths and Uncle Ben Hadad's discovery, and then my speedy banishment to Jerusalem where Gamaliel's influence would purge me from pagan defilement.

I look back not in anger but in pride as the Saul/ Paul I was then struggled for birth. Behind all this was my deep religious longing to love my God, Who in some way beyond understanding I knew to be at the heart of me and in some way at the heart of mankind and the heart of the universe. I watched the farmer plant the dry grain that could, by some miracle, be transformed from life in the dark ground, to the blade and then the ear of wheat blowing freely in the wind, then transformed by the grindstone, finally to be food for man and beast. The Osiris myth told of this miracle. Yet God was enshrined in the great Yahweh of Patriarch and prophet. He was deep-hidden, too, behind and within the Law given to Moses. We could also truly trace him throughout our Jewish history and we, the tribes of Israel, believed ourselves called, especially chosen, to lead the world to Him. What then of the great hierarchy of the Greek gods and goddesses? Was understanding of the many, many, myths another way to find God? Was He in the omnipotence of all-powerful Zeus? What of the worship of the Sun in ancient Egypt? And what then of my own personal reverence and delight in the human form? I had a powerful and pulsating desire to be united with, not the old Adam of Eden, but some new Adam, that Ideal Man whose strength I felt when wrestling and struggling, racing, leaping, outstripping. Was God to be found in the heights and depths of loving my fellow man and myself in him? Or was this powerful drive merely sexual desire? Was the Law really right and true, to harness and confine sexuality, to restrict and imprison such power and delight? Was it not originally made, given, by the Creator who made Adam? The Creator who gave Abraham the courage to leave his known world for the unknown and to father a nation, and to the prophets the strength to attack society? He who gave Moses a vision of the Law and gave me this longing to love to the uttermost?

I had, within me as a young adolescent, many gods, many altars, many longings and wrestlings, for and against many powers. As far as knowledge of the Law was concerned even my father could not fault me, though he was never fully satisfied, presumably because he suspected the hidden sides of me, un-imprisoned, unassailable, essentially part of my true self and beyond his control. Was he suspicious for fear of similar unconscious torments deep buried in himself? While I was young — for I was a child until that transforming experience in the Damascus wadi — I had been a slave to my father, though heir to all his property. I had been a slave to the Law, though, as a Pharisee, I had earned the right to be called Master of the Law. I was a slave to Rome, though a free citizen of Tarsus. Not until Love called me by my name did I know the freedom of being recognised and claimed as God's own son. Now I am filled with the same Spirit of Love, crying to God, as my lover did, "Father, my Father".

Freedom from Slavery

My writing in these last weeks has been totally given to recollections of my childhood and youth, those growing and formative years through the student days before and after I graduated in Jerusalem. I had such rich and varied and confusing experiences and I know, now, that the very confusion in which I struggled was the soil in which I had immense opportunities for growth in preparation for the overwhelming events of the last months and for what lies ahead. I may have repeated myself over and over in this journal for I have recollected and reviewed so much. Only in this way can I come to terms with and understand my new direction, my new goal; this sure climbing of the human soul by body to spirit, from the death and resurrection of the body to everlasting life.

The outstanding thing that I am now realising is that my Lord is clearly directing me to go back to the Gentile world I know so well — beyond Syria to Asia, then further, to Greece and, maybe, even to Rome itself. My way has been by Judaism, the way of a son of Benjamin, through strict teaching and training in Pharasiac Law. Now my way is the way of freedom through the revelation of Love Itself, the Father of all loving. The love that Jesus gives to me brings all the world into fellowship together in the Spirit of Love. God, Who is above all and in us all, is Love. What a challenge! But I can do all things through

Christ who strengthens me and enables me to carry out Love's will.

After the episode with the young Bedouin boy I spoke to Naboth about him. He told me that he was a slave boy called Timothy and he had bought him and his mother in the Damascus slave market three years ago. He had needed another shepherd boy to train up for lambing time and the boy and his mother were a bargain if they were bought together. Although they are Jews, the boy's father was apparently a Greek trader from Asia and had died of fever in Damascus. Even before the man died most of his property had been stolen by the servants travelling with him and illicit money was soon made, after his death, by this transaction in the slave market. But what was that to Naboth? He had paid up fairly and the woman seemed thankful and the boy content. The mother, Eunice, was a good worker and the boy quick and obedient and a remarkably good shot with a sling so that, for a time, he was nicknamed 'Boy David'. It was probably the Greek blood in him that had made the boy stand out from the others and had probably first drawn my attention to him.

I could not deceive myself that I felt no more human hunger for that boy. I was angry and disappointed when I felt desire arising in me. My love for my Lord was so intense, so all-absorbing, that I had felt it would have total dominion over me and physical hunger would leave me. "You are a man, Paul," I heard my Lord say. "I made you a man. Would our love destroy your manhood and have you less than man? Remember that I first loved you and you have no longer any need to seek for love. Timothy, too, knows your love for him and has no need for you to prove your love in sexual ways. You have told him that our Father's love is for him also."

Certainly, now, as the days pass, Timothy often comes and stands by me, or walks into Abila with me and when, in the evenings, I am telling young Reuben a story, Timothy and one or more of the children come close to hear. They bring their pipes with them and Timothy has made a lyre and plays tunes that delight us all — Greek rhythms, plaintive airs or old songs with refrains, as well as the Bedouin tunes they all know. It is becoming customary for us to gather before sleep for stories and songs and then Naboth comes and recites an evening hymn or a psalm of David and asks God's blessing on us all before we sleep. Though they know I am a rabbi and a Doctor of the Law they have their own pattern of family worship and never ask more of me than just the usual Jewish courtesy of the synagogue to strangers, "What have you to say to us, brother?" I am thankful for this, for I have no wish to assert myself over them. The hierarchy of the Temple in Jerusalem has no meaning for me now. I am servant to my Lord and share his sonship with his Father. I am neither more nor less than any High Priest or Levite, any shepherd boy or pagan King. We are all Christ, under Jesus, Christ, our Lord. I do not find it easy yet, to hold fast and remember this and the fact that the whole camp accepts me as one of themselves, neither more nor less, is a very great help to me. Of my trust in God as Love through Jesus I must learn to tell them.

My evening story-telling has purpose. Always, in allegory or parable, I speak to them of God as Father, Creator or Lover. "How do you know all this?" Timothy once asked and one evening young Reuben looked up at me and said, "Who told you that story?"

"A man called Jesus," I replied, "who lived once in Jerusalem. He tells me all my stories."

"What was He like?" Reuben asked and I knew I had been led to that point by the Christ Spirit in him and that my Lord was calling me to lead them to Him and so to God and the throne of Love in heaven. I had known the moment would come. I had wanted it but it was so important that I was almost afraid.

Slowly, surely, little by little, I told them not only the earthly story of Jesus — of which, in fact, I knew very little — but, more real to me, the story of my own meeting with Him and my learning that Love itself was, and has always been, my God and Father, holy beyond understanding and beyond the wisdom of all men and all ages. "I know it a bit," Reuben said, "from my father." And Timothy and I exchanged glances. We were all learning of Love, however faint were our earliest experiences. So I share my faith with them; a faith not learned by rote nor by Law, but learnt in our daily experience of living together. I tell them only what I know and only a little at a time and try to relate it to what they already know and they come back night after night for more and, lately, not just the children but often, the women, too, and the young men.

Yesterday evening, before sunset, Timothy came up quietly beside me and I noticed two women standing with their water-pots behind him, having just returned from the spring.

"Saul, sir," Timothy said, "the taller of those two women is my mother." I looked towards her and she turned away in natural courtesy. I only saw her face briefly and I had, of course, seen her often before without knowing she was Timothy's mother.

"Timothy," I asked, "what do you remember of your life at home and before you came to Damascus?"

"A great deal," he replied. "My parents had no other surviving children and I loved my father very much. He took me everywhere with him and when I was old enough he bought me a horse and I would ride with him. He had a chariot and would take me to the races and he would let me hold the reins sometimes when he drove. I stood in front of him and leant against him with my hands on his, not in a real race but when we drove round the arena practising. And he would take me to the agora with him and I would hold his money. And he would take me to the plays at the theatre, though that worried my mother. They went on all day and I often got tired, but I learnt all the old Greek stories and of their gods.

"My father could tell stories as you can," he went on, "but though they were more exciting than yours I couldn't really believe them. I like yours better because they feel true. Your God is kinder than my father's Zeus, who was often angry and frightening. I loved my father and he loved me and when you talk about the way you love your friend, Jesus and He loves you, I think of my father."

"Yes, it is like that," I replied.

"I wish he hadn't died!" Timothy said. "I shall always miss him and love him. I think my mother will, too."

"Real love never dies, Timothy," I said. We were silent till I said, "Do you miss Lystra and wish you could go back again?"

"Oh, yes, very much. One day I will buy my freedom and my mother's but she says that is foolish and we will never go back. I think my grandparents must think of us often. They won't forget. My grandparents bought my mother as a slave when she was only a child, so she knows about slavery. When she was old enough they arranged for her to marry my father. Her parents lived in Lystra but they were very, very poor and that was why they sold my mother. I hardly knew them for they died when I was too young. My mother is a Jew and has brought me up as one, too. My father let her teach me. He said it would do me no harm. She taught me herself as there were not enough Jews in Lystra to make up a proper synagogue, and no Rabbis anyway. I learnt quite a lot of the Law and I know many of those stories you tell Reuben and the rest of us. I like the way you talk about God much more than the proper Hebrew way and more than my father's way, too. I was really scared of Zeus and afraid he might come down one day from Olympus and I would have to meet him. But your God is Love and I understand that. I love you and I love your friend, Jesus, too."

The boy chattered freely but his words alarmed me not a little — 'the proper Hebrew way' he had said. He had put into words what was becoming increasingly clear to me, that the Way of the Lord Jesus was indeed a different Way, a different Truth, a different Life; different from the traditional Jewish way of which I was a teacher, of covenant and promise through a life of good works in obedience to the Law. My Lord's Way is through life lived on earth by faith in Love only, from the simplest beginnings in our relationships with one another to the giving up of mortal life as I saw for him on that hideous cross. Was it life or death that that cross showed me on that evening?

I had much to learn from Timothy's childish talk. He seems already to know what I had struggled for so long to believe. He learnt as a child to trust his father's love so he was ready and open to receive and give it. If we are open to love we dare trust our longings, follow our yearnings, for they are Love at work in us and they are the creative energy within us from God.

I am being so moved by Timothy's insights as we talk together that I now know what I would do. When I finally decide to leave this camp, probably moving to Gadara to cross Jordan and head for Jerusalem, I shall suggest to Naboth that I buy young Timothy from him and, if he would agree, his mother as well, and send them back to Lystra, to their home town and his father's house. He is half Greek and though his life here as a slave need not be unfulfilling for him, yet his mind would grow more in the city of his birth and with his own people. I have recently sold two saddle cloths to passing traders and another large camel cloth to a man in Abila. I sold my camel when I joined this family so I can probably afford the price of their freedom.

When I read this I seem just to be recording my logical thinking but it has been entirely in the presence of, and under the guidance of, the Lord Jesus. His close at-one-ness to me is so real and sure and the influence of his spirit so clear that I know even my smallest thought is in the light of his loving directing.

Once again I am awed by finding that the thoughts I have recorded above are an essential preliminary to the events of these last days.

Last night Naboth and I had been speaking of Eunice and Timothy and I had found him not unwilling to sell, at least Eunice, and we had agreed that son and mother should be together and there we had left it.

This morning an old, old man came to our camp asking for me. I was amazed, for who knows of me in these parts and how could anyone have found me? He arrived on a donkey, dressed in rags and with flies buzzing round deep sores on his legs and arms and back. He asked for me. "I am looking for one, Saul," he said, "who was in Damascus, a Jewish rabbi from Jerusalem." I went out to see who it could be, but could in no way recognise the old man. "Sir, are you the rabbi Saul from Jerusalem?" he asked.

"I am he," I replied.

"The Lord be praised!" he answered, and continued, "I bring you greetings from Ananias, your friend, also from Jerusalem and now living in Damascus. He has travelled south in search of you with a company of Jewish refugees returning to Jerusalem. He has traced you through those who remember travelling with you as far as the junction of the Raqqad and Yarmuk rivers. There he has been told you left the road that led to the Jordan crossing. He could find no further trace of you and there he is now camped. He has given me money to search for you and will give me more if I return with you. Though travelling with Jews returning to Jerusalem he is there only to trace your journeying and will not cross with them over Jordan. The company, in a few days, will cross over and he must then return to Damascus. Sir, he is very anxious for news of you. I have been three days searching for you, visiting villages and camps in every valley and wadi, and I finally heard of you in Abila. If you will come with me, Sir, I know a short route back to Ananias' camp that is only a day's journey from here."

I listened with amazement and delight. Ananias! My good brother Ananias! Brother of my Lord Jesus! He who had been chosen first to receive me, so soon after my first meeting with Love at the wadi outside Damascus. Perhaps he was even camped at that very spot! Ananias! Who had cared for me for Love's sake, though he believed me to be about to throw into prison those lovers of Jesus who had fled after Stephen's death. Ananias! Who had baptised me in the Damascus river and who knew me and loved me and accepted me as lover of the same Lord. He must have received my note telling him I had not crossed the river and so had come for news of me. "Naboth," I said, "I must go at once with this man. May I return to you in a few days' time?"

So, the old messenger was given food and drink. I gave him my second cloak and a fresh loin cloth.

"Could you spare Timothy to accompany me?" I asked, and, generous friend, Naboth immediately called him and told him to have a camel saddled for our departure next morning.

How strange and marvellous are the works of Love. Again, in the night, Love spoke directly and clearly to me, not in words, but in the creative Logos, the Word of God, incarnate within us. In the innermost depths of my soul I knew what I must do.

How the disciplined trained rabbi, Saul, would once have accused himself of blasphemy for framing his thought in that way! But I sensed in myself part of the Creator's Plan which I was to bring about and when it was achieved I would behold what Love had done and see it as good. Rabbi Saul bowed before Brother Paul, the new man, who in releasing the young Timothy from human loving freed him for the purpose for which Love had made him. Love called me. Love drew me. Love acted through and in me.

Next morning I rose early and called Naboth from where he still slept. I offered him a price for Eunice and Timothy. I offered more than he had paid for them and more than a fair price for he had trained them for his service. I asked him to let them go with me to the camp where Ananias waited with the company returning to Jerusalem. "I cannot pay you until I return," I had to tell him. But the Christ Spirit worked in him as well as in me and, after talking together, he agreed. He sent for Eunice and Timothy and I told them I had bought them, not for my service, but that they might travel with me to join a company travelling to Jerusalem. From there they would journey to Antioch in Syria and then, under God's guidance, back home to Lystra. I did not plan this as I used to plan my campaigns for persecuting the Jesus followers or as I planned my visit to Damascus or as I used to scheme and plan my visits to the Roman barracks or even as a boy, my escapes from home to the back streets of Tarsus. I only knew that I was working Love's will and it was right and real and good. There was a peace and joy within me that the world cannot give as poor Eunice fell at my feet sobbing, her scarf hiding her face and unable to look up.

"Take your mother away, Timothy," Naboth said, "and prepare her for the journey. You must leave before noon."

Eunice got to her feet and Timothy put his arm across her shoulders. He is already as tall as his mother. He led her away without looking back. He must have found it hard to believe what he had heard, but I felt sure that there would be joy in his heart too, for he knew now of my love for him, and that that love was the Love of God, his Father, in whose hands he was safe.

First Ambassador

We were a strange small company. The old man led us on the donkey. I rode a camel loaned from Naboth. Eunice was behind me on a saddle bag with our loads on the opposite side. Timothy ran alongside or climbed up on the donkey behind the old man, whenever we could make good speed on an easy part of the track.

It was a rough road but a beautiful one. We went up wooded slopes and then on to the pass over the hills and down to join the broader track through Wadi Shallalah till we reached the Yarmuk. Here the river meanders until we saw the waters of the river Allen tumbling down the hills from the north to join the Yarmuk. It was fortunate that we had the old man as our guide for he was able to take us to a place where we could cross the river by three small bridges that spanned the rocky boulders where the river twisted and turned. Our camel was reluctant to cross, but men from a nearby village, with cries and shouts and waving of arms persuaded her with dignity to risk her life and we crossed safely. The donkey minced its way quietly over, ears pricked, and Timothy scrambled over the rocks. We stopped on the farther side and ate dried figs and apricots and drank milk. I spoke to Eunice for the first time.

"Eunice," I said, "You do not know me. Your son has tried to find in me a lover and a father, and I have tried to turn his love for me to love of the

Father of us all, Love Itself, under Whom you and I are bound together as brother and sister. You need not fear for you are led by Love and Love will be with you every step of your journey."

She did not look at me as Timothy could have done. It would have been unseemly in a woman. I could not know how she felt. She had known the uncertainties of slavery and, for a short time, the security of belonging to a husband but there had been little security in her life.

"Your son will be with you, Eunice," I went on. "He knows God's Love for him and he will tell you how we share a friendship with a Lord and Master, the Messiah, of whom our Jewish prophets spoke. The Messiah has come and I am close to him and speak in his name. The Spirit of Messiah is in us all as I and your son Timothy know, though Timothy has not yet fully grasped what this means. In his newly found freedom he will come to know that Love, Who is our God, is born in us. Love is with us and we know this through Jesus, our Lord and Christ."

She glanced quickly at me, puzzled and bewildered. I could say no more. I did not know what I had said and I listened to my own words, not fully comprehending. A seed was planted by the spirit of Jesus, by Love, in Eunice and in me to grow secretly and I left to my Lord the growth and the flowering.

We sat quietly, saying nothing, watching the Yarmuk waters tumbling on their way, over and round the boulders in the wadi. Timothy, loins girded, feet bare and legs and arms dripping from the river, scrambled up and sat by us.

"Saul, sir," he said, "I will miss you. I shall hear no more stories and how can I remember all about our Lord Jesus, your lover, if you are not there to remind me?"

"Because, Timothy," I answered, "you will need no reminder for our Lord is going with you. I will not seem far away and I believe we shall meet again. Nothing can separate those who are brothers in Love's family. I shall probably one day return to Tarsus, the home of my childhood and if you reach Lystra, it is not far away and I shall visit you. I shall long to see you. Come, let us go on, I wish to reach Ananias to-night."

So we continued our journey and the old man was excited and called to the people as we passed through the tiny villages, "I've found him!" — for he was retracing his steps by this time — and they called back, "Shalom!" "Thank God!" and "The Lord be praised!" and shaded their eyes to look up at me, the stranger on the camel with the woman behind him and the young boy on the back of the donkey. The village children ran after us shouting and the hens and sheep scattered before us.

I thought of the rage that had filled me the last time I had journeyed towards Damascus. I had been impatient then as now, but then I hurried to exterminate the lovers of Jesus, blasphemers and law-breakers, who threatened my peace. Now I was impatient to reach Ananias and my impatience was full of joy and eager anticipation for I had found peace.

I am writing this a week later and am now back in the camp with Naboth, Reuben and the rest. I brought back with me two young men who had travelled with Ananias from Damascus and who knew Jesus and who wanted to go to Derla and then on to Baghdad. Naboth might have been glad of them for a time. If he wished, I had told them, they could travel with him, helping with the sheep. If not, they could travel on alone.

We had arrived at Ananias' camp perhaps an hour before sunset. "They are still there!" our old friend shouted when he saw their camp ahead and not far off the road. As we came closer it was clear that much packing to move off had been done. Ananias came out to meet me and the warmth of the meeting was so genuine that I, tough young Saul, so easily full of hate and rage, was in tears! Judas from Straight Street had come too and several of those returning to Jerusalem whom I had known in Damascus. Some were still a little unsure of me, I felt.

"We had thought of you so much, Saul and were both overjoyed and surprised when we received your message. It had not seemed possible when you left that you would disappear for ever, though you were in no mood when you left us to return to Jerusalem. When we heard you were still east of Jordan we decided to come as far as this to see if there was any news of you."

The worst of the persecutions in Damascus seemed to have died down and those of Jesus' followers returning to Jerusalem were going back, mostly, to do business or see to their farms or to collect their belongings, children and family and then they would probably return.

I explained to them that I had bought Timothy and his mother out of slavery for Timothy had found his Master in Jesus. I told them the story of his Greek father's death and their being exiled from home.

"Stories like this are common in Damascus," Judas said. "It is one of the crossroads of the world and its population always on the move. Tragedies like these are daily occurrences." What was so surprising to me was that there seemed no need to explain to them what I had done or why. We all knew, through the Spirit in us, that events were taking place around us and a wordless plan, of which we were a part, was unfolding. It needed no exertion of human will to bring events to pass, but rather a submission of ourselves, our souls and bodies, to Love, as we learnt it through our Lord.

It was stimulating and refreshing to be back again with lovers of Jesus. They talked so much of 'Jesus said this . . .', 'Do you remember when he did that . . . ?' 'How he said when he was among us . . .' The assertive dominant side of me was longing to say, "Don't hold to the past! He is alive! What is he saying to you now?" And I must admit that it was hard not to be envious as I listened to them for they had known him in the body. But it was good to be with them and share, not merely their talk, but Jesus himself. The memory was with me of that dead but never lifeless body, limp on the cross. I saw there the ultimate submission to Love, the ultimate acceptance, the immense strength of spirit in that bodily weakness and final surrender. That was my only experience of my Lord in life but how precious a symbol it was of all I knew him to be. So I held back as they talked and listened and picked up as much as I could of all he had said and done when he lived among them.

Suddenly, a young man whom I did not know came up to me and said, "Brother, did you say that the mother and son you had bought out of slavery were from Lystra?"

"Yes," I replied.

"I am journeying," he said, "to Jerusalem. I am in the leather business and am returning from Damascus, which is the end of my trading journey, back to the centre of our family business in Derbe. From Jerusalem I must go to Antioch in Syria, then on to Tarsus and through the Golden Gates to Silicia and to my home town which is very near to Lystra. Your freedmen could travel, if they wished, in my care." I was amazed. Ananias, only an hour before, had given me money specifically to give to Timothy and Eunice. Their journey was opening up, a smooth path before them and I knew how, for Eunice, this would seem a miracle. Indeed, it was a miracle; a miracle of understanding love shown by this Greek stranger and by Ananias and me, all of us caught in the Love that cared ceaselessly for His children. I had never before known power at work like this.

Here I must record another miracle, a strange and private one. At the back of my mind, ever since we had left the camp and throughout the journey, a troubling thought had stirred. I would not let it come to the surface to be considered but I was restless and it would not leave me. Love's plan was surely unfolding for each of us but, I wondered, and fear had filled me at the thought, was I myself, even now, to join this company we were so soon to meet and return with them to Jerusalem? My return one day is part of the plan for me. This my Lord has made clear. But, had the moment come? I was afraid. Afraid of returning. Last time my Lord had turned me back, saying so clearly, "Not yet!" This time there was no clear word or order. Was I now to go? Where would I go in Jerusalem? They would not trust me yet. Not to Gamaliel. What could I say to him? Not to the barracks. There would be ridicule to face and perhaps temptation. I could not suddenly leave Naboth for I had told him I would return. My parchments, my cloak, my weaving materials were back at the camp. I could not leave that group of friends who had been so generous to me without a goodbye. Yet was this the moment when I should go since there would be friends to travel with and Timothy and Eunice to set upon their way? I worried and planned and thought this way and that, thankful when the thoughts were pushed aside by the events of the journey.

What a fool I was! All that restless, hasty scheming and worrying! Had I learnt nothing? Had I no faith in my Lord? Was I still unable to trust his love and place myself wholly in Love's hands and know the peace past all understanding and plotting and planning?

Oh, what a fool I am! Jesus did not speak to me this time in a voice that said "Not yet!" but in the voice of the unexpected traveller from Derbe, in the money Ananias gave me for Eunice and Timothy, in the natural unfolding events. This was my own private miracle. It was clear to me that it was not my planning that was necessary but my acceptance that Love's plan would be, was being, fulfilled in, through and for me. My Lord was leading us all as surely as if he had issued orders. My fear had gone. Peace returned. My life in the hands of Love is blessed. I am so slow to learn, so swift to act but faith and trust over-rule even me and all is over-ruled by Love.

Ananias, Judas and I, with a few of the others stayed awake much of the night talking. I told them that I was to be sent to the Gentiles rather than the Jews. I had not realised how hard it would be for them to accept and understand this. It is so clear to me but I should, with my Rabbinical training, have realised how deep rooted in Judaism they were and how hard it would be for a traditional Jew not to think of our people as a specially chosen people and Gentiles and pagans as beyond the reach of the Love of God. I am beginning to see with increasing clarity that we must make a decisive choice as to whether we please God most by what we do or by trust in His Love. I have in myself such deep-rooted habits of making decisions about what I must do, how I must act, how obey the Law, or, equally decisively, how break it – the good Jew! – that it is hard to put myself wholly in the hands of Love, though I love my Lord with a devotion never known before, knowing he loves me always and I never have to win his love.

When I left Damascus I had felt totally cut off from the Jewish community there. The traditional Jews were deeply suspicious of the new thinking and teaching of the Jesus Way and had hoped, when the letters I had brought from the Sanhedrin reached them, that they would have a strong ally in me. They were naturally appalled when they heard I was no longer a persecutor but a new convert, a follower of the Way. The followers of Jesus, on the other hand, especially those recently arrived from Jerusalem were also deeply suspicious of my change of heart. Either I was infiltrating their ranks to spy or I was a sentimental, emotional hot-head! I was, to them all, erratic, unstable and untrustworthy, except to Judas and Ananias. So I had left Damascus thankfully and in perplexity. My world was turned upside down and I had felt outcast from the Jewish refugees, from the regulars of the local synagogue, as much as I must be, now, from the Sanhedrin in Jerusalem.

Since I came away I have been, in fact, a solitary. I have met splendid people, much hospitality and generosity and I have had time to come to terms with my new Way and, above all, to come closer to my Lord and through him, to know more and more that Love is my God.

Now, Ananias and Judas had left Damascus to search me out. It was marvellous of them to come and amazing that they found me. They said it had not really been difficult for my movements had been noticed by many people for various reasons. Rumours had followed me from Damascus; people had noticed small things — my scrip and wallet, my parchments, my foreign sandals and cloak. Some had noticed that I spoke Greek and Hebrew and Aramaic and some remembered actual things that I had said. "We could recognise the voice of the Lord Jesus" Ananias said, "in many of your words that they quoted to us."

"We couldn't let you just disappear, Paul," Judas said, "as if you had never been, as if we had never met you through our Master and were not therefore closer than any brothers who shared an earthly father."

Certainly, in that evening we spent together, Jesus was with us and we shared his spirit again, saw each other through his eyes, loved, knew and respected each other, as he loved, knew and respected us. "Saul," Ananias said, "we wanted to find you to tell you this. Whatever persecutions, hostilities, troubles lie ahead for you and there will be many, we know Love has chosen you for His service. You have been commissioned through His son, Jesus, to carry the Love of God far beyond any of the visions of our prophets and mystics, far beyond the dreams and visions of any faith and age, to the ends of a world greater than our imaginings. Bless you, brother Paul, go out into the world in peace, in the service of Love, our God and Father, in the power of Christ within you and in the holy spirit of all the children of Love."

"Not many in Damascus trust you, Paul," Judas said. "They are still too full of fear." He went on, "Fear of the fate befalling them, that befell, not only Jesus but Stephen and other Jesus lovers, those whom you had imprisoned. In time they will understand and one day you must return. As love becomes perfected fear will go."

Dawn came and the party, with Eunice and Timothy, prepared to move off and join the many others on the road to the Jordan crossing and beyond. It was strange and sad but clearly right to watch Timothy, my son in Christ, move off with strangers. My last words to him were, "Judge your own conduct, my son, not that of others. Carry whatever your load may be with courage and faith and remember always that Christ is in you and you are in the hand of Love, Who made you according to His will. Go, now, in the name of our Lord, Jesus, the Christ."

A chapter was ending and another beginning and we shall meet again, maybe on earth, maybe in heaven.

The Past Relinquished

Ananias, Judas and their little company were also to leave, returning to Damascus. Our meeting had been brief but so abundantly blessed that our parting this time was in peace. There was no anxious fear as I had felt in our last parting. We would be close in the spirit of Christ, even when the whole world divided us. They had come in search of me purely to assure me of their love for they knew that I would need friends and supporters in the days ahead. I was deeply moved and as in turn they took me in their arms in farewell we knew that Christ was with us in power.

When they had turned round the shoulder of the hill and disappeared I realised they would soon pass the wadi where I first met Jesus face to face. I was left with the old man and the two men who were to return with me to Naboth's camp. The old man soon left on his donkey and I found the men were willing to delay our return until the next morning. I was glad for I needed some time alone. I had much to think about. Ananias had revived such memories in me. Many sayings and events of Jesus' life were retold last night and I wanted to store them safely in my mind. I needed to review the private miracle of how my Lord had made me aware of Love's will for me. Timothy's departure and my relationship with him needed time and quiet. I had much to absorb and accept.

The men went into the village to find a room for the night. I left the camel with them and walked up the side of Mount Hermon and looked down on the dusty road.

On looking back on those hours up there I do not know whether I was in the body or out of the body, on earth or in heaven. I looked down on the people below, of whom I was one, to whom I would go and yet I knew I belonged to another world, another Kingdom, a 'Kingdom of Heaven', of which, Ananias had said, Jesus had often spoken. In this Kingdom of Love there were no citizens, slaves or servants of the King, as in the kingdoms of this world, but all were heirs, children of a King Who loved them as a Father.

Below me, as I watched, pilgrims, Roman militia, traders, returning travellers, crowds, in both directions were moving along a highway of the world, while I in the spirit looked down on them. Many stopped at the roadside booths near the village and bought food and settled in families or companies to eat and spend the last night before they reached the river crossing. Most of them, I supposed, would travel on to Jerusalem and some would go to home towns in Galilee or even further south or west. Children were chasing each other; women in bright colours were crouched round cooking pots or carrying jars of water on their heads or hips; men were squatting under the trees, sharing a smoke or a drink or news and others sat at tables in the shade of reed roofs watching the crowds and idly gossiping. Donkeys brayed; sheep, tethered at door posts, bleated mournfully, and mules and camels were tied together with one or two small boys keeping watch.

Each one of those people below me, I mused, is an

idea from the mind of our loving Creator, each one is beloved of our Father God. Each one is filled with Love's Spirit but they do not know it, do not see each other in the light of the Love in which Jesus saw them all.

My thoughts flew back, as I watched them, to the thirty-two years that I had lived. Desires, longings and lusts had driven me to search in those around me for reflections of myself and love of self had been as far as I had ever reached. I had longed to see in myself the innocence and charm of my young cousin Isaac; the grace and beauty of Silvanus at the Tarsus games; the energy and devotion of Stephen, right up to the moment of his death; the dignity and dominance of Cyprian, the centurion from Macedonia. Many of my youthful lovers came to my mind and I remembered how I had longed, by every human means in my power, to be in union with them and by mutual love share with them the qualities I so much admired. Self-love had driven me! As, in the Greek story, Narcissus had loved his reflection in the water, so had I loved myself as reflected in my fellows. Clumsy, unhandsome Saul, despised and despaired of by his father, often ridiculed, even by those he loved, yet seeing himself at one with all the beauty and grace and power around him and striving with single-minded devotion to find fulfilment of his desire and hunger for love from them!

The Jewish Law saw nothing but sin in my lifestyle. All my study of the Law pointed to my guilt and condemned me — covetousness, gluttony, idolatry, lust! Without the Law I would have known no guilt, no condemnation. After hours of study I would see my sin so clearly and long to lay it on the back of some scapegoat and drive it away from me, to die in the wilderness with its load of guilt.

"Enough, boy!" I remembered my father saying as darkness fell. "This is to be memorised by morning," and my lesson over I would leave my room, get food from the servants, drink and shower myself at the well and go out, scrambling over the roof, into the town. In a short time any scapegoat for guilt was forgotten and I was back in the agora or the circus watching again for beauty of form, virility, strength, the bright eye, the broad shoulder, slim hips, muscle of thigh and limb, the wrestle, the race — the longing, never fully fulfilled, to be in union with all those gifts of beauty and so come to love myself as I saw myself reflected in other men.

Then came the revelation, recognition, realisation of Jesus. His wretched, blood-stained body had haunted me with a guilt I dared not face as I had seen him on the cross. The justice of the Jewish Law that I had learnt and struggled to obey, had killed him, for blasphemy, for he had said he was a child of God and I condoned his death. He was dead and I hounded his followers to their death to fulfil the Law, prove myself its advocate and so satisfy my pride and confirm my superiority.

I can laugh now at my pathetic longing to love and be lovable. I am still utterly stunned by the realisation of the love he has for me. It blinded me. "Why?" he said, "You persecute me and hound me to try to prove that I cannot love you to the uttermost! My love for you will never die. You are a child of Love, made in the image of my Father. How could my love for that reflection of my Father ever die. I, too, can never die. The death of the physical body is no death. It, too, will rise again. If you bury a fruit it will rise to new life, another form of the same idea, transformed, reformed, refreshed, renewed. Saul, I love you. I have loved you since time began. You are sincere, single-minded, honest and faithful. Always you will go for the highest when you see it. I will send you, ambassador of my Love, not merely to fulfil the Law but to fulfil Love beyond the Law, to reveal to the world's end, the union in Love of Everyman with the One, in Whom we live and love and have our being."

Small wonder that even while I remembered these things I realised what great courage I would need to cross the new Roman bridge over Jordan and make for Jerusalem. How could I ever face Gamaliel and the Sanhedrin on the one hand and the friends of my Lord who had lived with him on the other, with this message?

There was jealousy of Jesus' friends still in me. They had had three, perhaps more, years of close friendship with him, day in, day out. I had had one timeless moment, and that moment not of time but of eternity. They had lived life with him, heard his 'blasphemy' and experienced his death under the Law. I had never known him in life and could only share with them the horror of his dead body. Yet I knew, more surely than they, the power of his resurrection. I thought again of Gamaliel and how faithful and diligent a Pharisee and teacher he had been. I thought of my years of struggle with the Law in order that my actions and activities for God would fit me for some far away heaven, where I might sit down with Moses and the prophets at last – exhausted, I expect, by my efforts! – all a cover-up of the truth I now know. I am loved of Love and so free to love my fellow men.

All these thoughts came to my mind on the side of

Mount Hermon, as, wordlessly, my calling became clear. Jesus, my Lover, was sending me, Paul, to the ends of the world, to the end of time, to give my gifts for Love to every human being. Love of my lesser self died and was resurrected as love of the Greater Self, the Christ in me, free to love all Love's children.

No wonder, at first, I was blinded! I had never been loved before. Not for what I truly was. The Narcissus image was drowned and resurrected in the Light of Love. So, during those days of blindness, surrounded by the gentle care of first Judas and then Ananias, I had come to the truth that God, through Jesus, loved me.

I knew my return to Jerusalem from Arabia would come. I was ready, almost longing, to go and only awaiting my Lord's word or his sure sign. The Sea of Tiberias lay ahead, the river Jordan lay deep in the gorge below, the new bridge hidden but I knew that before long I would cross into Judaea and the journey would begin that would take me over the Great Sea to — where? Cyprus? Asia Minor? Greece? Even to Rome itself? I would go out, no longer in the pride of Pharisee, a Benjaminite, a circumcised Jew, nor as the seed of Abraham but a son of Love, the God above all gods, glorying only in the mystery of a crucified body, a resurrected Messiah, alive for me and in all people for ever. But again I knew, "Not yet!" and thought of Timothy and Eunice, still, probably, trudging that dusty road on the first day of their freedom, journeying in Love's care. Truly Timothy was my son in the Lord.

So, through the rest of that day I wandered over the hillside and as the sun moved fast towards the western horizon I sat under a thorn tree, going over again and again all the events of my life, which I now saw as miracles of coincidental interweavings which had brought me to that moment in the wadi on the Damascus road − not far from where I then was.

I watched sandy hills, rocky ravines and distant mountains change from the harsh browns of the mid-day sun to the gentle blues and mauves and haze of evening. Then, when the sun had set, before darkness fell, the sky turned fiery red and suddenly, in its dying rays, I saw again my Lord on the cross, a cross stretched and elongated, reaching out across the sky until it overhung the earth below and the figure hanging on it reached out as if to embrace the universe and then faded and then in the silence, clearly, wordlessly, he made his purpose clear and I understood. The time had not yet come to cross Jordan but I was to put away all thoughts of the past and reach forward to all that lay ahead. The purpose of the past is accepted, recognised and understood. I need dwell on it no longer. I must move forward to fulfil the high calling of Love, as a runner races towards the goal. My heart sang! Fear and guilt were cast out again by his love! I saw! I knew! I leapt down that hillside in near darkness, boulders falling all round me. I jumped down the dried up stream beds, scrambled down screes and ran over the grassy slopes where the wild flowers laughed up at me in the last of the light and my feet crushed the herbs and the air around me was filled with the scent of thyme and marjoram and lavender. The ending of that day, seeing my crucified Lord embracing the world in the rays of the sunset spoke to me of a chapter ending and a new beginning.

I reached the road and, more slowly now, thinking

deeply, walked in the dark into the village and soon found my companions. They had had food prepared in a hostel and we ate in the courtyard by torchlight.

"Tomorrow we go back to join Naboth's camp," I said, "and in a few days I must pack up to leave them. I shall journey first to Gadara. Probably I shall then travel south by the King's Highway, visiting some of the cities of the Decapolis on my way. You are welcome to accompany me or to offer yourselves for hire to Naboth to help with his flocks if your plans are better served that way. When you meet him and discuss matters you will be able to make your choice." So we slept, and in the morning journeyed back to the camp.

Into the Future

"... the not-yet in the now,
The taste of fruit that does not yet exist,
Hanging the blossom on the bough."

Laurens van der Post

"METAMORPHOSIS" - Oil - 36" x 48" - John Reilly

Gadara

I am writing this now in the city of Gadara where I have been received into a delightful Jewish family who, when I asked whether they had room for a stranger, offered me hospitality generously. The walk here had been pleasant, first down to and across the Yarmuk river and then up over the hills and finally through the wooded country of Gadaritis to this town, built imposingly, on a stony broad plateau from which I can see the Sea of Galilee in the distance. I have rented a comfortable room above a colonnade of shops, for my Jewish host is the town baker and his oven and shop is below me. I look out on the street, full of activity and bustle. Several young boys and girls go in and out, pushing through the crowds with baskets of bread on their heads which they sell in the streets and lanes and roads around the town, returning for more when their baskets are empty. "Eager servants!" Simeon, the baker, laughingly told me.

There is plenty of noise below, but I am writing on the roof above my room for there is an outside staircase leading up here and a rush shelter gives shade from the sun and catches any fresh breeze. Here I am at peace.

It was a wrench to leave those Bedouin friends. They had accepted me as part of their community and I believe they would have been content to have me travelling with them for as long as I wished.

After I ran so joyously down the slopes of Mount Hermon that evening, after Ananias and Judas and I had parted, the next stage of my journey had opened up clearly before me. I must prepare myself thoroughly and carefully for what lies ahead for I see clearly the wisdom of my Lord's instruction that I should now look forward and no longer look back or dwell on the past. There is much about which I am still unclear and no student who has sat at the feet of Gamaliel could take any message to the world until he was totally convinced of the truth and logic of his insights. I have to work out clearly where I stand regarding the Law. I have not had those years of study merely to reject it. I cannot easily discard what I so much respect simply because I have been given a new vision of Love.

Then, also, before I set out as the ambassador for my Lord I must raise my love of mankind above the mortal to the spiritual. Often in myself I still feel the difficulty of curbing physical lust and sexual desire. Up here on the roof I have spoken to my Lord of this. "You will have this natural hunger always, Paul." He tells me. "It will nag at you like a thorn in your flesh but my strength is greater than your weakness and through this very urge you will find a sensitivity and understanding of your fellowmen. You will be alongside them in their battles with mortal hungers and desires and you will, by the strength of my love, raise them to fuller life." I hold on to my Lord's words but much here still troubles me and I have much to think through and learn. What of my fear of women? Would perfect Love cast out even that fear? Yes, for Love which is my highest Goal, my God, will so fill me that I will fearlessly embrace the world, far beyond Jordan, that wide world over which the arms of the crucified had been spread in the sunset on Mount Hermon.

After several days I have begun to know Gadara fairly well. It is an impressive, ancient and historic city, renowned for its great learning. Some say it is the greatest cultural city of the Decapolis. It is very widespread and has three theatres, a splendid temple, many springs and a reservoir. Because of its springs they say the place must have been inhabited from before recorded time, first as a camp, then a simple village and now as a thriving town. The house where I am staying is in the Jewish quarter at one end of a long colonnaded main street which is also the busy market area. The baker, Simeon Bar Jonah, with whom I am lodging, is an elder of the synagogue and it was because I was a Jew that they were glad to welcome me and I easily felt at home with them. I had not been a welcome member in any synagogue since I left Jerusalem and it restored my confidence to find myself accepted among them. There is a large congregation and at Sabbath worship, when they realised from my dress that I was a Rabbi, I was not only invited to speak, an opportunity they would probably have given to any stranger, but I was asked to read from the Law. I was deeply moved when the Torah was taken from the Ark and carried, with solemn, somewhat noisy, chanting and bells ringing, round the congregation. This was the Law which had been my God-given goal. This was the word of God inscribed 'in my head and in my heart and on my strong right arm' as the phylacteries symbolised.

"Thou shalt have none other gods but Me."

"Adonai! Adonai!" they chanted. Then came my turn to read from the Psalms of David. I had a job to hold back the tears as I read the passage Simeon directed:

"Oh, Lord," I read, "how I love Thy Law! It is my study all day long!" (Indeed, it had been my study, day after day. I had learned to respect the Law as God's Word but I did not love it with the love I now have for my Lord, Jesus, Messiah.)

"I have more insight than my teachers." (Ah, there I spoke from the heart. Insights are given me from my Lord, far beyond anything I learned from my teachers.)

"I set no foot on any evil path." (I? Who had suffered torments of guilt because my feet had been set on every path the Law had taught was evil!)

"I do not swerve from Thy decrees." (How often have I swerved! How could I read that?)

"Thy Word is a lamp to guide my feet and a light on my path."

Surely they must have heard my voice tremble as I read and I could only just hold back the tears as I returned to my seat. In the synagogue at Gadara that Sabbath day I had been brought face to face with the Law in the presence of my Love. The Torah and the crucified Messiah. The prayers and the ritual continued as a noisy, muddled background to my thought.

"Thy Word is a lamp to guide my feet and a light on my path."

Yes, that was what God's Word in the Law had been in the past for me — a lamp guiding me in the darkness, a light shedding a beam on my path. But Love's words to me had been a Light that blinded, a flood of Light, bright as the noon-day sun, that dispelled darkness and shadow. In Him is no darkness at all. He is the Light that lightens every created being that comes into the world, Light above all light, Love above all loves. I an not in darkness but in the light of Love and Life.

I have studied and loved the Psalms so much over the years that, back up on the roof, with the street quiet down below and stars sparkling in the sky, I recited the whole of the psalm of which I had read a part in the synagogue. Strangely I found myself remembering the children in Naboth's camp in the evenings when they brought their pipes and drums and lutes and made music. There was an old folk-song that a young boy called Isaac sang, which had a refrain. We would all listen to his young treble voice, free and happy and rhythmic. At the refrain the goat-skin drum and the lute would join in, and, as the song went on and on, other instruments or other voices would be added but it was young Isaac who set the pace and tune and we followed his lead. Love sets the pace and tune and is the free and happy leader and the Law is the follower. Love is the rhythm. The Law can harmonise but not create the tune. We are the followers of Love's leading, each of us a separate instrument playing Love's tune. Love is engraved on the heart. The Law is engraved on stone. Love draws mankind in faith to God. The Law orders men to obey God, commanding the community to conform, punishing disobedience.

It is in this synagogue of Gadara that these thoughts have come to me. I am being brought face to face with my, as yet unsolved, problem as to whether the gospel of Love replaces, transcends, fulfils, or abolishes the Law. How I long to stand up in front of them all and confess my faith in the crucified Messiah, tell them he is here and the virgin birth of the spiritual man is revealed through Jesus, my Lord. I am not yet ready to proclaim this. I am strong in faith and in love but not intellectually yet able to place Love in the context of the Law and show that Jesus is Messiah, the fulfilment of our Jewish destiny, calling us to be messiahs with him and take our places in his kingdom of Love.

At the other end of the Gadara colonnade is the magnificent temple to the Goddess of Love and this I also reverence though Jews throughout the world are in opposition to pagan worship. It is this opposition that binds us, as uniquely chosen people, to our one God, Yahweh, above all others. I am hearer and learner more than ambassador in these days in Gadara. I return to my room or up to the roof above and there I sit studying as earnestly as ever I did at the feet of Gamaliel in Jerusalem. Every thought is captive at the feet of Love. The power of Love builds up and does not tear down, creates and does not destroy. In the past I used my authority and power to tear down and destroy but now my faith in Love gives me strength to build up and create in His Name.

It is several weeks since I last wrote my journal. It is now the first day of the week and the Sabbath has just ended. Rabbi Simeon asked me to address the congregation this morning in the synagogue. It was a privilege to be asked and it would have been discourteous to refuse. But how unsure I was. The courage with which I had first spoken in the synagogue in Damascus had gone, for then, even with Ananias, Judas and other lovers of Jesus to support me, I had experienced the hostility and suspicion that had made me leave Damascus. Here I was alone.

"Lord, what am I to say?" I pleaded.

"When the time comes, Paul, you will know what to say for I will speak through you."

Strangely, when I had finished, I had not known what I had said and cannot even now recall my message. I felt like a potter's vessel that has no idea for what purpose it is to be used or what it will pour out.

"The Kingdom of heaven is at hand." I heard myself say. "You need not climb up to heaven to find the Word, for it is already in your heart and you may hear it and do it. You may look and not see, hear and not understand, give honour to the Word and deny it in action, or understand it and still disobey."

The Word of which I spoke was Love but I dared not utter that greatest of all the names of God.

Afterwards many of the congregation thanked me for my words and my insight but all I can see before my eyes is Jesus, the Christ on the cross and Stephen falling on his knees. I am ashamed. I, who had always prepared my preaching with such logical, meticulous scholarship and pride, I am ashamed. I will never preach again until I can speak openly and unafraid of the crucified and risen Messiah, revealing Love to mankind. The words that came from my mouth this morning were given to me and they were hidden from me, for there was still in me the fear of my fellow men. It was a fear that I had felt after I preached in Damascus — that old fear of being rejected and unloved, scorned and undesired.

For ever I shall remember Gadara as the place where I was shown clearly that Law is not at war with Love. The conflict of the two has been in me. The Law has been a school-master to lead me to Love; a discipline to lead me to freedom. As Moses received the Law from God to lead unruly, untrained Israelites from bondage to the Promised Land, so now, the modern Israelites for the second part of their Journey, have been given Jesus, the Messiah, to show them the Love of God, to lead them from the Land of Promise to the freedom of Love's Kingdom of fulfilment. The Law does not go far enough but Love fulfils its purpose. The Gentiles to whom I will go will not and need not know Moses' Law for their faith in the love of Jesus is shown by their willingness to be 'crucified with him' — that is, die to the mortal body and be raised a spiritual body. This is the way that they must follow, as surely as the Jews have followed the Law. The discipline and training of the Law comes from the mind. The discipline of Love comes from the heart. How can a lover covet or steal from, be envious of, or lie about the beloved? Whether that beloved be fellow man or God? The Law enslaves us. Love frees us. Those who prefer the formal discipline, the imposed moral code of the Law, cut themselves off from the free, self-discipline of following the Christ within to the heart of Love. Law is for the citizens of earth. Love is for the citizens of heaven. My Lord has called me to turn from my past and press on to fulfil my calling and in my weeks here in Gadara I am learning how to die to the Law and live in Christ. The time seems now to have come to leave. I have learnt here more than I ever expected. Much from long talks into the night with Simeon. I am ready now to press forward and travel south as the Spirit of Love will direct. Perhaps I shall not cross the river until as far south as Jericho for still I feel sure I shall be called to face the apostles in Jerusalem before I shall be ready to travel further afield.

To-day I told Rabbi Simeon that I would soon move on. I was restless last night wondering if it was cowardly of me to leave that congregation before I had told them that Messiah had come and of the death of Jesus and the power of his resurrection and of his revelation of Love for me. "Paul," my Lord had said in me, "as you learn to trust my love for you, you will no longer judge yourself by the Law as 'brave' or 'cowardly', 'right' or 'wrong' in speech or action. The old Law is done away. Because you have faith in Love, I am in you and you in Me. Whenever your thought or action is directed by Love for any of God's creatures you are the Christ, obedient to Love's calling and seeing through Love's eyes. Here lies the salvation of the world. This is the power of Christ."

By early this morning I was calm again but forced to realise that this soldier of Christ was not yet ready for the battle-field. I am, piece by piece, putting on the armour of Love — the shield of faith, the sword of Love's spirit, sandals winged and ready to go. With these I am equipped but I still seem to lack the courage to fight. As I now look forward I see the task ahead as a real battle, not against human-beings, Love's children, in His image, my brothers and sisters, but against the world's values. It is these that are at war with Love; false gods, false doctrines, low levels of loving, poverty, disease, materialism, these are like poisoned arrows and deadly spears, to wound and weaken even those to whom Love's power has been revealed. All the energy I once gave to wrath and envy, hatred and condemnation must be totally diverted to the service of Love. I long to fight. I am armed and ready. Here in Gadara I have held back the full confession that Messiah has come in Jesus, crucified and alive as Love. Only when I confess this will I be able to fight boldly in his Name. Yes, my Lord speaks clearly. I am a soldier in training to fight Love's foes — all the lusts of mortality, for money, possessions, power, self-righteousness, all of these bow down to love of self. I will fight and proclaim to the world the love that Jesus, the Christ, has shown to me. I am as ready to die for him as were his lovers whom, in the past, I had flung into prisons and dungeons and who died at my hands. But death has no dominion over Love, so rather than die I will live for him, Christ in me, to be glorified for ever. What holds me back?

Yesterday morning early I went down to the market. I needed an animal for my journey and decided to review the market prices. I would be travelling mostly by the King's Highway and a horse would serve me better than mule or donkey and though more costly, it would be less expensive than a camel. There seemed nothing there to suit me. "So what,

Lord?" I said in my heart. As I turned away a man, another Jew, greeted me I recognised him as a member of the synagogue whom I had met briefly at Simeon's house and I spoke of my problem. How often do I find that Christ in another meets my needs and in such unexpected ways — ways I would never have found myself. This man knew a man to whom he was speaking last night! He had told him of a man, well-known in Gadara as hiring out carriages for travel on the Highway, who had got seriously into debt and whose usurers were threatening to take him before the judge to force him to pay. He was hastily looking for purchasers for one of his carriages and two horses. So this casual meeting with a near stranger directed me to the man's courtyard and I had soon arranged purchase from him of a strong, well-broken horse. He was full of relief and gratitude for I finally gave him a rather higher price than he would have got in the market and, for me, it was considerably less than I would have had to pay with little time to haggle for a quick sale in the market. So I now possess a good bay mare with a white star on her forehead, broken in and well used to being handled. Also she can be stabled with the man from whom I bought her until I am ready to leave. 'Sheba' she is called and I rode her into the hills around Gadara in the evening, thanking my Lord Jesus who, in this way, had made it so clear to me that I must move on and had provided me with the way of doing so.

I will journey south towards Jerash and Philadelphia, ready always to turn west and cross Jordan river and travel towards Jerusalem as Christ in me makes my way plain. I feel that Arabia and especially these towns of the Decapolis, being Greek and Roman as well as having Jewish communities, will give me the feeling of the Gentile world in which my life-work is to lie, and the journeys between them in the hills of Gilead will give me the solitude I need to be alone with Jesus. Daily the Christ in him and the Christ in me are becoming one. All the self-confidence I had through my knowledge of and attempted obedience to the Law of my rabbi days has been broken down. Instead, my confidence is being built up newly, slowly, surely, in union with Jesus, bearing fruit as Christ. I glory in nothing but Jesus Christ crucified and Christ in me, my hope and joy.

Yesterday was the Sabbath. Earlier in the week I had told Simeon that I would be leaving on the day following and I am writing this journal from a camp I have made for myself between Gadara and Pella. Simeon, when he heard I was leaving, begged me to address the congregation once more before I left. I did so. Christ guided my words. I chose for my theme the passage that was due to be read that day — "By means of people speaking strange languages I will speak to my people," says the Lord. "I will speak through the lips of foreigners." I begged them to be open to the Word of God coming to them, not only from prophets, teachers, rabbis and learned men but to their own hearts in visions and words from God given to them and to them alone.

"Watch for the Messiah in your midst," I heard myself say. "The Laws of God were written on tablets of stone but the Love of God is found only in your hearts and lives. You are called to be prophets, fore-runners, revealers of the Messiah, for His day is at hand." I told them that I who came, a stranger and a foreigner to them, had been shown, through them, truths of God's Love for His creation that were more wonderful than I had dreamed possible. These wonders were revealed to me, not through my studies of the Torah but through my love for God, Who speaks to me through my fellow men, foreigners, kinsmen or strangers, as well as my own countrymen.

Further than this I could not go but a very old Jew took my arm when the noisy singing and chanting had ceased and said, "Truly God is here among us."

"He is in you, old man," I replied and loved the Christ I saw in him responding to the Christ in me.

I returned to Simeon's compound, awed, with a full heart, for I had come nearer to speaking boldly than before and had felt no fear as I spoke. "You are the Christ," "Love is the fulfilment of the Law." These are the truths that I have learned in Gadara. Christ in me. The union with Love is complete. So, this morning, I collected Sheba, returned to the baker's house, loaded my goods into saddle-bags bought in the market, mounted, and with Simeon and several of his family and children from the bake-house to lead me to the end of the colonnade, I passed through the Great Gate, bade them farewell and left Gadara behind me.

I did not intend to travel far and soon after mid-day, turned off the straight road to Pella to travel by hill paths. I have food and a fire-pot with me and am now settled for the night under trees, a little way from the hill path. There is a small trickle of water in a nearby stream-bed, sufficient for Sheba and me. Simeon had given me bread and meat and a small oil lamp, very old, dug up amongst some old Greek ruins, of Greek design. It is made as a small man, or small god, leaning towards the flame warming his hands or perhaps he is shielding it. It burns surely and by its light I am writing but will write no more. Is that small man myself, warming myself at the flame of Love and shielding that Love from winds that would extinguish it? The flame, the light of Christ?

Sheba and I woke at dawn. I have let her loose to crop the grass, nuzzling among the wild anemones, marigolds and daisies of the hillside to find the creeping clovers and new grass amongst them. It is chill and I draw my cloak around me and listen to my Beloved. "Beware of boasting." He said. "Don't think of yourself as better than others. Each of you is different and each is uniquely beloved. Judge yourself only against Love. If you follow natural desires that is the harvest you will gather. Sow in the spiritual field and you will reap a spiritual harvest of love, joy, peace."

Such calm has come to me that I have decided not to journey much further but to spend another day and night here in the hills. This afternoon a flock of sheep rounded the hillside led by a young Bedouin man and his much younger brother. They watered the flock in the wadi by my camp and the older brother stopped to talk to me while the boy brought in the straying sheep. He wanted to talk about his problem at home and found I was ready to listen. He had recently been given a wife and after a few short weeks of living with her in his tent she had become cold, silent and withdrawn and he could not reach her. Clearly he was, by nature, gentle and kind but he was tempted to enter with physical force, subdue her and make her his but something in him recoiled. I told him what I now know, daily, with more and more certainty, that you can judge no one else's conduct. Only Love can truly understand and that, not by mere human loving, but with that Love which I first knew in the Damascus wadi, the Love of my Creator who made me as I am. True love, I told him, accepts totally, not what might or should be, but what is, now, which is the one moment when time touches eternity. Physical desire, the meeting of his own needs, made that shepherd long to force his wife to accept him. His loving concern was not for her. Love of self motivated him for his own pleasure. If he sows in that field there can be no harvest. If his love is for the Love of God within him and in his wife the seed he sows will live for ever. He need not, must not, compare himself with other men — those other young men who boasted to him of their conquest of their women. He told me he looked at the other young girls as yet unbetrothed and longed to take them. I told him how well I understood his temptation and then of Jesus, now and forever my Lord, far above all the powers of heaven and earth. He looked at me in amazement. "He is the Messiah." I said. "He was killed by men's desire for power, by the might of Rome, by the Law of Moses, by the self-love of the princes of this world and I was one who agreed to his crucifixion. But he has shown himself alive to me and I am now learning to live in the light of his life and love for me which burns within me."

I spoke of my faith and hope and love of my Lord but am still unsure of how to speak of this to others.

Probably my words puzzled him though I spoke, being alone with him, with more confidence and, now, after he has left me, I know I can trust the Christ in him to take whatever Love would reveal to him from my words. Am I irresponsible, to trust my Lord so surely? How far am I responsible for what I say? Would Gamaliel rebuke me for speaking of the deep things of God without due preparation? Yes. He would say that the Word of God must be spoken with awe and reverence and never given without being framed in an atmosphere of prayer and due reference to the Law. Was I now free to leave my words to frame themselves, in faith in the Christ in me? No. My disciplined life and respect for the Word finds it hard to allow this. If we are called to be preachers and teachers, we must construct our thought with care, using words with understanding, fully aware of their meaning, knowing how they can mislead or be misunderstood. Unless we do this we cannot call ourselves fit to be teachers or preachers. I believe I am called to be teacher and preacher and have been given the gift for this work. Feeling this deeply, as I do now, I offer this gift to my Lord, to use in the service of Love and vow to use it only when I am close to him. I know the responsibility of serving Love in this way to be far greater than being a teacher of the Law or the prophets. This I learnt and had confirmed in Gadara.

This morning as the sun rose and Sheba grazed quietly — I heard my Lord say, "Go in the Name of Love, and tell every nation of the Love beyond Law, beyond any Promised Land of the Jews, beyond the Great Sea and the heights of Olympus, a Love that reaches beyond sun and moon and stars and sky, Love that is the Creator of all that is made. You are more deeply and truly my beloved than the wildest mortal dreams and desires you have ever experienced. I pour every spiritual blessing into your heart and as I have lifted the world above the slavery of deceit and hypocrisy, so I would lift you to be a saviour of the world. I am in every corner of the world and I send you to reveal the Christ, in the Name of Love, the God and Father of us all."

I heard these words in awe and rose to my feet, gathered my things together, shouldered my pack hastily, threw my sheepskin over the saddle, leapt on Sheba's back and galloped up through the trees to the crest of the hill where the path turned to descend. At the top I paused, for below me lay the great city of Pella.

Pella

Right across the hillside the great city stretched but dominating it all was a great temple and below it, carved into the hillside, a theatre, with a tiny spiral of blue smoke still rising from the altar. Below me the light of a new day sparkled on the river that ran through a narrow gorge from the hills, opened out as it reached the gentler slope and then circled the town and the sun rose, golden, on the Greek columns and Corinthian capitals.

I gazed and gazed and then looked down and saw beside me a small Bedouin boy. He was looking up and staring at me, his dark, shining eyes gazing intently and a frown puckering his brow; but there was no fear in his gaze. I leapt to the ground and flung my arms around him, hugging his beauty to me and tears poured down my face. My tears alarmed him and perhaps also did the strength of my grip and he struggled free and ran up the hill, turned and waved and then disappeared among the trees. A little kid ran after him bleating anxiously.

"Thou shalt have none other gods but Me." These words of the Law rushed to my mind. How true they were. The gods of the world were ranged before me — Ra, the Sun god, Artemis, goddess of chastity and hunting, Beauty in a small boy, all the world's idols and artifices, and the Law now dead to me. Life had gone from it for I lived in Love so that there could be no thought of divided loyalty or other gods. All were one through Jesus my Lord, and by his grace, my allegiance was only to Love, his Father and mine, his God and mine.

I mounted Sheba again, turned back towards the Temple and, quietly, as the sun rose we descended the hill, slipping on the steep gravel path and trampling on camomile and rosemary so that the air smelt sweet with herbs, till we reached the river. I let Sheba drink her fill and then crossed and spurred her up the steep hill to the foot of the Temple. We clattered up into the town, past women descending with water-pots and bundles of washing and children running ahead and alongside, until I was beneath the pillar of the agora.

There were two men, educated Greeks, I could see, sitting together on the steps. They stopped talking and hailed me. "Welcome, stranger," said one, "in the name of all the gods be welcome! I see your saddle cloth is of Damascus weave and your horse is not of our breeding. Have you come from far?" He spoke in Greek, so in Greek I replied.

"You are right, friend. I have travelled from Damascus, though my home town is Tarsus in Silicia and I am a Roman citizen of Jewish birth. Thanks for your welcome. I left Damascus some months ago for Jerusalem but am in no great hurry to return having personal problems to solve before taking up my work again. So I am, at present, travelling east of Jordan river and visiting cities of the Decapolis before I finally cross to Israel and Jerusalem."

"May the gods and the stars guide you," one of them replied, "and, if you wish to stay, my home is open to you. I, too, have personal problems and destiny often helps us solve these things by sharing them."

We talked politely of this and that and relaxed, and I felt their welcome was warm and genuine. My mind was full of my new awareness of Love; indeed, my thoughts as I travel are of little else. Will I be able to share my experience with them?

Pella is a splendid city. It is essentially Greek, in culture, language and religion and is, in fact, the first almost totally Greek city I have ever visited. Tarsus was too much at a cross-roads between east and west and being a port as well, was multi-cultural. Neither Roman garrison nor modern buildings imposed on ancient ruins, nor even the wreck of a very old Phoenician ship in the harbour, a danger to the fishing fleet and the Roman navy, could over-rule its Jewishness and its vigorous Jewish syna-gogue. Damascus was a trading city, linking east with west and Jerusalem was always the Holy City of the Jews. But Pella has no port and the town has grown there because of its springs and its river and the forests on the hillsides. The trees are felled to make masts for the Roman navy and poles and parts for chariots and it has a thriving industry in these things.

My friends in the agora told me all this about their city and I was glad to accept the hospitality of the older man, Cirius. The younger one, while Cirius was talking, had left us and gone down to the theatre to place more incense on the altar and blue smoke rose, waving gently into the quiet air of the early morning. He was wearing a Greek robe with a deep purple border over a Roman army tunic so I supposed he must be a Greek belonging to the barracks on altar duty for that period. Cirius and I

112

watched silently and all was quiet save for the morning sounds of an awakening city, sheep bleating, a donkey braying, a child crying and others calling as they ran down to fill water-pots from a spring and then carefully climbed up the hill again, the jars on their heads. The market was coming to life behind us, goods were being displayed as shutters were opened or removed and we could hear the feet of pack-animals bringing wares from the country. Leather goods, sandals, cloth and pots were sold in one part and fruit and food-stuffs, meat and dried fish in another.

"Tell me of the gods you worship in Pella," I said, as Justinian, the young lay-priest rejoined us.

"They say," he answered, "that this city, for many, many centuries has worshipped the Sun-god and right to this day we venerate the Sun. It is Artemis who is the supreme guardian goddess of Pella and this altar is dedicated to her. She pours on us great blessings, filling our forests with bear, wild boar and antelope and giving us generous grazing on the hillside."

"There are nymphs and dryads in our waters, too," Cirius went on, "that give our spring waters healing powers."

"What gods do you worship?" They asked me.

I told them I was a Jewish Doctor of the Law and was instantly ashamed. It was an empty boast and was the answer I had always given until this last year and came out thoughtlessly. It did not answer their question and told them nothing of the God I now worshipped. "But," I added hastily, "I mislead you by answering your question in that way. The true answer is long and difficult but if I may accept the hospitality of your house I will have time to tell you and would gladly do so."

"That we shall look forward to with interest," Cirius replied, "for Greeks, as I expect you are aware, are avid for knowledge of the gods for each one leads us one step nearer to understanding the mysteries of birth and death and the destination to which we are all bound.

"Let us go up to the city," he continued. "Your horse can be sheltered with mine, and my house is available for you to use as you would your own."

So I made my first contact with Pella and I have met that same open warmth wherever I have been in the city. The people seem genuinely to welcome strangers and be interested in all that is new and different as well as being a community close-knit in the worship of Artemis.

I am being given most generous hospitality in Cirius' household and was instantly made welcome. I still had an unopened wine skin from the vines at Gadara and gave it to them to show my gratitude and they set olives, dates, almonds and figs before me and apricots and peaches dried from their own orchards. Certainly Pella is a warm-hearted, peaceful place to find, probably because, being predominantly Greek, it has no conflicting cultural clashes to cause division among them. Visitors, strangers, traders are all made welcome without fear.

"It is Artemis who holds us together as one people," Cirius said.

I thought instantly, 'They love and trust her and are therefore bound to one another in their love of their goddess. This is the way for them, until they add to it the Truth that Love is the one God and there are no others. Will I be able to tell then that this Love is revealed in the resurrected life of Jesus?

Tell of Love, the Father above all?'

I have plenty of time here for writing as I am alone during the days for both Justinian and Cirius have their work to do. Justinian is an orderly in the barracks and Cirius has a large timber trade business working with two of his sons, both married and living in the same compound as their father, their houses on the two other sides of this courtyard. I wander in the market and then saddle Sheba and ride up to the most northerly part of the town, to a hill where there is a ruined temple of many years ago. From there I have a view not only over the town but away to the west, across the rift of the Jordan river to Galilee, the land of my Lord and lover. Then I look towards the south-west to the mountains of Samaria and see Mount Gerizim rising, the highest of them all, hazy in the mist. All my learning of the Torah and of our history comes back to me. That mountain stands, to the Jews, for the fulfilment of God's promises to His people, a reminder of His blessing on those who obeyed and His curse on the disobedient. To those who obey will be given all the blessings of God's chosen and beloved.

'Write the words of the Law on your door-posts and gates, teach your children, bind them on hand and head and heart and speak them in and out of your houses when you lie down and when you rise.'

There has always been, amongst us Jews, this sense that we have a strange, sure, destiny as the People of God. Our nation, our religion, is built on this. The Messiah we await is expected to be another individual prophet in the great succession. We have been so used to great leaders — patriarchs, prophets, kings, the great heroes of our history, that we seem unable to visualise anything coming from God in other than individual form and following in that succession.

All this I had learnt from my youth and all this I had cast aside for a more excellent way – a Way that fulfilled all the Law and the prophets – the knowledge of God's Love for me in the face of Jesus Christ. Jews are a practical down-to-earth people. Not for us the gods of myth and legend, of Olympian heights, or depths of Hades but I now know all these insights to be made one by Jesus on the cross, as love pulsated in him even as his body died. Friends and foes alike abandoned, denied and rejected him but love for all men, from Love Itself, lived on in him, beyond death. This is the Reality, the mystery, of heaven and earth, where dreams and visions and daily living are made one. Can this pagan city prove this truth to me?

In Pella there are two strangers who are generously offering me the hospitality of their home and who, perhaps this evening, certainly within the next few days, will say to me, "Tell us now of the gods you worship." How shall I answer?

I am unchangeably and always loved and Love is the God I worship. Each day I realise, more and more, that this unique and personal love of my Lord that I can experience only between him and me is freely available for everyone – Jew, Greek, slave or freeborn, man or woman. I also know that I cannot yet totally trust myself to be as true to my lover as he is to me. I might still be carried away by my older lesser loves, my self-loving hungers and desires. That great load of memories from my past still pricks my conscience and is not totally stilled. Yet I am accepted as I am, was and will be and I marvel at this and long to share this truth with others, until we all are made one in the Christ that Jesus revealed.

I stood on the hill above Pella again this morning and looked across Jordan towards Jerusalem and Israel and suddenly, with something near fear in my heart, realised how much I was giving up. That great body of the Law, God-given, tried and tested, that I had learnt with such diligence and had studied for so long, I was casting aside for a man who loved me. I was fearful. Mount Gerizim, towering in the distant haze, symbolised the Law, immovable, unchangeable, eternal. Had I really thought through what it meant to give up that security, that sure foundation thrashed out and forged throughout Jewish history? How long I remained there I do not know and then, quietly, surely, the Christ in me revealed the truth — "Neither to the mountains of Samaria nor to the Temple in Jerusalem need you go to worship Love, Love reaches to the uttermost parts of the earth and in Spirit and in Truth before the mountains and the hills were formed He loved you and will love you to all eternity. Trust Love."

My Lord Jesus was very close to me but I realised I would find it far easier to tell those of Cirius' household of the Law of Moses than of Love! I had been trained to frame learned discourses and had no fear of logical thinking. I could expound the Law with skill and ease and I could see Cirius calling for more wine and Justinian stifling a yawn! No! Love was my God and theirs as well and together we would share and learn of Love and I would tell them only of Jesus, my Lord and glory only in the Christ, crucified and resurrected. I would speak to them of what I knew and not of what I had learnt. I laughed as I realised how reluctant was Rabbi Saul to give way to Paul, the lover!

Sheba tossed her head and whinneyed as if she were laughing too and she brought me back to earth. Once again I knew that through the whole unfolding of my life, what God was showing me was Love and as each experience came, the hard and difficult, the good and beautiful, through pain and joy, yes, even through anger and fear and jealousy and despair and misdirected zeal, Love's purpose was unchanged and I was beloved.

"Right, Sheba," I said. "Back to the city! You, beloved horse and I, beloved son. Each of us part of the world Love made and I, in His image."

It was as I suspected. After the meal that evening fresh lamps were brought in and we were reclining on the couches with cups of wine. The servants and women had retired. Justinian and two soldier friends of his, Cirius and his sons, Glaucus and Marcus, were with us and an older man of the household they called 'Uncle'. Cirius said, "Now, Paul, answer for us the question we asked you soon after you joined us. Tell us of the god or gods you worship as a highly educated Jew and Doctor of the Law."

The way he opened up the conversation made it difficult for me. I had to begin in a negative and contradictory manner.

"Cirius, my generous host and all of you who hear me, I must first explain that, though it is true that I have studied Jewish Law under the greatest modern scholars in Jerusalem and have obtained my degree in Pharisaic Law and am by birth a Jew and the God I love and worship is indeed the God also of the Jews, I have learnt to live by another Way shown to me by a young man called Jesus who went through death just two years ago at the hands of those who despised and hated him. He is my closest friend and my lover and my Lord."

Justinian interrupted. "But now dead, you said?"

"No," I replied, "death could not hold him. He is alive and for evermore my Lord, and through his death and resurrection he has led me to the One God above all others, Love Itself."

It is certain that I held their interest. They were startled and puzzled and I, who had thought that a negative start, the denial of my old allegiance to Pharasiac Law was an unfortunate place to begin, was suddenly glad it had gone that way. Now that these men knew that I had a scholarly background and an academic discipline and training it would be easier for them to hear me out when what I had to say might well make them sceptical and scornful and ready to ridicule. The laws of hospitality would not allow them to show this and they listened carefully to me. I told them my story shortly but emphasising the tensions of my double life with my Jewish upbringing and Greek/Roman social background. Then, with confidence, I told them of my meeting with my lover and Lord in the wadi on the way to Damascus.

"Paul, your story rings true," Marcus, the older of Cirius' two sons said. "My search for love and fulfilment has been in the pursuit of women. In many of them I thought I had met the final end of my search only to be frustrated and disillusioned and often disgusted at the dashing of my hopes and my endless hunger for satisfaction. Then, a year ago, I was betrothed and then married to a Greek girl sent here from Macedonia, where part of my family

119

lives. She had been orphaned and my father was anxious to help the family where he could. He sent for her and offered her a place as a servant in our household. Soon after she had arrived I realised I wanted her as my wife and with my father's blessing I married her. With her I have found a love and understanding undreamed of before. Because of her, Paul, I understand your faith but, though I find in her a grace and beauty and understanding undreamed of before, will this last? My wife is not very strong and has frequently been ill since we married. If she should die, love will die with her, only a memory of our love will remain and that will fade. If, as you say, Love is God, above all others, supreme, how can we grasp and hold Love in this life and not merely know it so fleetingly, an unrealisable hope, a longing, a distant goal, a dream, a vision, without hope of actualisation? It is so fragile, so precious, so short-lived. You seem to have found a Love beyond life and death."

The love of which he was speaking was a love I had never known. "Marcus," I replied, " your love for your wife is real and rare and is a milestone on the path of your journey, not your goal. It measures the distance you have travelled and points towards a goal which must be no less than Love Itself. I would tell you more but it is getting late and I would tell you about Jesus, my Lord, not so much my love for him as his for me and how it is that he has given me a peace that is beyond human understanding. I will leave you now."

"Paul, tell us more tomorrow," they begged me and Cirius led me to my room, called a servant to bring me a lamp and bade me goodnight and the blessing of his gods "and the blessing of your Love-

God, too," he added and then left me. I fell exhausted on my bed. I had been brought face to face with the love of man for woman. I had never known this love and yet, as Marcus spoke of his love for his wife, I recognised at once that this was the same love from God that my Lord gave to me.

"Lord," I called. "Lord Jesus, receive my spirit! Come close and hold me for there is a struggle in me that I can neither understand nor face." I struggled to keep sleep away, for Marcus' sincerity as he spoke of the love he knew was so real and I recognised it and yet knew nothing of it and wanted to understand. Yet, try as I might, I could not stay awake and fell into a deep sleep.

Then all at once that old dream came back to me. I was fighting again the battle of Light against darkness but I recognised and loved the Light and the darkness turned, like thick black smoke and writhed and cringed before me and then dissolved and faded and I woke and watched the dawn break into a new day and I knew the Christ again within me. "My presence is always with you, Brother Paul," I heard. "You know me. You know who I am and you have found the Love that is God in me, through me to receive and to give."

Then I saw, whether as vision or as waking dream I cannot say, a great mass of water, the Water of Life, living Water, flooding over the universe, then breaking into vast rivers, falling in great cascades or spreading in gentle ripples, round rocks and over boulders, into crevices. and bays, reaching all created beings. It was the Water of Life, carrying Love and Light to all the corners of the world, revealing Love in innumerable forms. And I heard the voice of my Lord saying, "You are carried in the mainstream of Love. You come directly from the Source and Father of Light and Life, in Whom is neither shadow nor darkness. You are learning that Love reaches each of us in many different forms, not only as Creator of the universe but Preserver, Lover of all things. Learn of me, Paul. Learn of the Christ in your brothers and sisters, in meekness and lowliness, and you will find there is no end to Love's revealing and I am with you, the Christ, everywhere and always."

Marriage

Next evening, when I joined Cirius and the other men after their day's work for bread and wine and meat at the end of the day, Marcus called one of the serving girls over to us and said quietly, "Paul, this is Phoebe, my wife." I was captivated by her. She is very beautiful, coloured as the anemones, with deep dark eyes and she wears scarlet and apricot colours, stitched with gold under her white veil. She serves me first as the guest and as she places the glass bowl by my side a scent of herbs wafts over me and her fingers, her hands, the movement of her arms, captivate and hold me and I feel a power and heat in me drawing me towards her. She then serves her father-in-law and then her husband. Every time she serves Marcus I notice her arm brushes his shoulder and his hand moves out to touch hers and place the bowl at his side. I see the brief touch, no more, of their fingers. I am jealous. Yes, I want someone to serve and care for me as Phoebe cares for Marcus. I have to admit a fear of her as I must admit a fear of all women which began with my fear of my sister when I was a boy and the absence of caring women in my life and my ignorance of their place and role amongst us. But Phoebe? Could I ever break through to a woman? To one special woman? One who would love and serve me as Phoebe loves and serves Marcus? One whom I could look at with the reverence, trust and delight that I read in the looks and touch by which Marcus shows love for Phoebe, his wife? Yes, I am envious. I see Phoebe through Love's eyes and watch her every movement whenever she is with us. She fills the water-pot in my room and, for a moment, I an alone with her. I think of Marcus and how he is entitled to be alone with her night after night. I think of them together and of all they can share and learn and discover. I try to visualise myself as a husband, a father, as having made a woman pregnant, not just to satisfy human desire but as a consummation of a rich, deep, sharing.

I feel, as I write and think these things, the heat and energy that I have known so often in my hungers after men and it disturbs me. Then, like some overwhelming storm, the thunder breaks, the lightning flashes, ceases, rain falls and tensions are relieved and I return to myself. I know my only love is for my Lord. Am I the woman and he the man that I give myself so wholly, body and soul, to the Christ Spirit poured into me? Can I bear in my body the fruit of his penetration? He first loved me. He came to me, seduced and captivated me, and his love for me and mine for him has in it a sharing and a learning and a trust in God as Love that is more profound and everlasting than any human symbol can express, whether by a wife to her husband, or slave to his master, or the mutual sharing that I see there is between Marcus and Phoebe. The love I see between them is, nevertheless, a more real and sincere and close expression of human love than I have seen before. My love for Stephen, Barnabas, Simeon, all my lovers of early days was good, honest and true. Yet how clearly I see now that it was self-love that motivated us, and we gratified our love of the lesser self in our sharing. Love can perhaps be expressed at greater depth in the self-giving of man in harmonious relationship with woman. This I see in Marcus and I believe he recognised the Love of which I spoke when I first spoke of Love as the God above all. I will never know love as he knows it. My fear of woman stands in the way. No one knows more surely than I that perfect love has no fear, seeks no power, looks always at the beauty of the Beloved and gives, totally. I know this in Jesus' love for me which nothing human can surpass. Because of this my hunger is over. Lust is the hunger to be loved. Love hungers only to give with no return. I am given Love from my Beloved, so hunger for love no more, but long only to give what I have so richly received.

I must record a day in Pella when Marcus and I visited Hassan, an older cousin of his. He had two wives and three small children and they came in to greet us. The women brought in a brass tray and set it on a table with wine and fruit and nuts and sweetmeats, indicating the special nature of the occasion. I watched the women with interest and perplexity. What can one learn from them? How understand them, except in their subservience to men? How fathom the mystery of them? They fascinate me, in a fearsome way, and while their quiet gazelle eyes are still vivid in my memory, I muse, pen in hand, and must write about them.

On reflection I realise it is not about them that I can write but about my attitude to them. I find a guilt remaining in me, a guilt associated with my sexuality, a writhing of my mortal body where I had thought it dead, nailed to the cross of my Lord. The old nagging thorn in the flesh. I recall again my early years of childhood and adolescence and understand that these experiences conditioned me beyond the control of reason, though reason now gives me understanding. I had no mother to whom I could relate, and a sister who showed me no love, and over all, my father, remote, devoted, curious, over-anxious and a stranger. The threshing of flax, care of the animals, work on the looms was for men; the girls were grinding, cooking, sweeping and rarely came my way. Much time was given to learning in the synagogue or from my father, who, ambitious for me, demanded that more and more of my time should be given to this study. When, at last, he would release me, I was off to rejoin my gang of friends, not merely Jewish boys but boys from the barracks, children of slaves, a motley crowd from Greece or Syria or Asia Minor. Girls looked shyly or slyly on, a species that seemed as different from me as the donkeys or camels in the streets. Then came adolescent awakenings, comparison of prowess with other boys and stories of their sexual conquests with each other and girls and women. Then, one evening, by the river, young Stella, older and taller than I, a Greek girl and an easy conquest among my friends, taunted me, caught me by my belt and tried to disrobe me. I was terrified and repelled and a negativity seemed stamped on me and I fled from every female encounter to the uninhibited pleasure and freedom of my male companions. Any guilt recalled by the teachings of the Law was easily pushed aside by my fierce emotions and troubled me far less than my fears of femininity. I did not, and still do not, respond to the soft and yielding physical form in the feminine as I do to the splendid male physique and strength of muscle in agility and athletic movement. Women are passive and subservient and men active and assertive. I am essentially active and outward-going, quick in movement of body and brain, repelled by withdrawal and passivity in myself or any other person. But I never won in physical contest as a boy, for though I was stocky, strong and muscular, and with stability, I had not the speed and dexterity of movement that I so much admired, to be a winner. I wrestled as well, physically, when I was younger, as I wrestle now in words. On looking back I cannot think that there was much to be physically admired in me. I was the admirer!

Once again, as I write, I feel myself looking back at another person. Was that child and youth to grow to the man I now am? Was that child, that youth, floundering through the waves of life, the beloved child of his Father, God, now lifted above the waves? Is my body as I know mine now to be, truly in subjection to Love through love revealed to me by Jesus, my Lord? I know my experience of life as I now live in him, in Christ, means I need prove myself no longer, neither by skill of mind nor body, by knowledge of Law, by understanding of secrets or mysteries, by skills of music-making, wrestling or chariot-racing. Already, I am loved and honoured, and without love these things are of no value. Nor need I now give my body to the burned and so purge myself of desire. I am ready to throw away abilities or possessions by which I may boast of my worth. I boast of nothing. I desire nothing save to glory in the love of my Lord Jesus, for, in him, Love embraces, honours and accepts all men everywhere, and women too. This truth, this marvel, is daily more sure and clear and as the Christ was revealed in his lifetime by Jesus in Galilee and Judaea, so must the Christ be revealed in me, here in the wilderness of Arabia, these cities of the Decapolis and later, I feel sure, beyond Jerusalem, Damascus, Syria and Tarsus, through Asia Minor, Greece, maybe to Rome itself.

Then there rises up before me, not just my lover of the Damascus wadi but strangely, vividly, that dead body of my Lord, a living symbol on the cross of the death of the mortal and the resurrection of the spiritual, a death I share with him that I may also live in him.

I think, then, I shall never marry. To be unmarried is, for me, a more excellent way. I have met my lover, surely the most faithful and true and I, too, would be faithful and his willing slave for ever. I could give myself to no other human, male or female, but only know union through the Christ in me and everyman. This means I shall neither be a mortal husband nor shall I father a mortal son, but I would, by Love's grace, through Christ, be father to all his children and brother to all His sons. Yes, I would be father to them and mother, too, for as the Greeks speak of Athena, Mother of all, so I know Love to be our spiritual Mother and we, as it were, Virgin born, brought to birth, nurtured, nourished by her through the power of Love Itself.

Three days have passed as I have thought more deeply, in the light of Christ within me, of the love of man for woman, of the powerful mortal sex-drive that brings them together and without which we would never have known the relationships of father and son, of mother and child. Marcus knows a mutuality of giving and receiving in his marriage that can perhaps be known humanly in no deeper way. I recognise it as deeply symbolic of the love of my Lord for me, but my Lord's love is no symbol. It is reality, understood, recognised, only by and indeed because of the death of his mortal body at his crucifixion. In that death of the mortal is revealed the Spiritual force of the universe. Death of the mortal, that we so easily fear, has no power over Love.

It was because of this thinking that, as Marcus and I walked the hills together yesterday, beyond the city, I said to him, "Marcus, brother in love, you fear the frailty of human loving. You fear Phoebe's physical frailty and the death that may take her from you, and this torments you for your love is human. Perfect love casts out fear. The God who is Love has neither beginning nor ending. Love loved you and Phoebe before the world was made, and will love beyond your death into eternity. He has given you to each other for your understanding of Love. It is the eternal Christ in each of you that sees the other in love as my Lord Christ sees and knows me in love. Phoebe, Marcus, Paul must die to the mortal that the Spirit of Love itself may rise, liberated, enriched, and incorruptible. Enjoy to the full the knowledge of earthly love you share and know, that, in Christ, the seed you plant in her body to bear fruit in this world, bears fruit in the World of Spirit as Love."

I did not preach this at him. It emerged between us

129

in the give and take of conversation. I heard and learned as much as spoke. We shared and set each other's thinking free. When I was alone again I was strangely glad that I would never marry. Love, as revealed to me by the Lord Jesus, was, it seemed to me, more direct and real for there was no intermediary. Sex in every union reveals either lust or love in endless human terms and variety. Union with Christ Jesus bears fruit in the Love that is God.

Since writing the above I have written nothing for five days. My stay in Pella is being so full and important that I seem now to have little time to write fully for every moment alone must be spent close to my lover and Lord. No studies of the Law in Jerusalem in my student days were as demanding as these days here. I will try now to record jottings of the last days so that when I continue my journey, as soon I must, I may look back carefully at what has happened.

Five Days Ago
The men gathered round me that evening in the courtyard and I could see three or more strangers in the shadows. "We have our own god of Love, Eros—" they began and I stopped them to speak to them of the earthly man, Jesus. 'Love incarnate', I called him. Then I spoke of my early search, as Marcus had searched. I spoke of my longing and vision, of my search through philosophy, history, ethics and the Jewish Law, and of my failure to find satisfaction as

I searched for love among men. Then as I told them of my meeting in the wadi on the road to Damascus. I could sense the Christ speaking through me to each of them. I knew he was alive to them. He gave me eloquence and sensitivity and imagination to speak of a truth deeper than I knew and words were given to me.

When I came to the point in my story where my companions helped me onto my horse and led me, unaware of the world around me, to Judas' house in Damascus, a silence fell between us. Then I said quietly, "I will not tell you more tonight." I had met Jesus, who had been crucified, whom I had seen dead on the cross, and I had learnt through him of life beyond bodily death and knew through him that I was loved of God, regardless of apparent doings, wrongs or failures, because I was made in His image. My vision was real and my search was ended and Love brought me into union with him! I rose and said quietly, "Love is with you and in you too and blesses you," and moved towards my room. One of the strangers followed me and gave me a lamp at my door and said,

"May all the gods bless you, master!" and I was alone with my Lord.

Four Days Ago
We were full of relaxed gaiety and trusting warmth today. Glaucus and Marcus and I rode over the hills to a point where we could see the Great Sea beyond Judaea and we galloped back with a delight in health and strength. That night I told them how I had seen Jesus' mortal body, dead, and how I had

come to understand its symbolism — the sign through a mortal man, of total giving of Love in life, in death and into the timelessness of eternity. Again I knew the Christ reaching those men and me also, as I heard his voice through me. He made it increasingly clear that the cross on which his human life seemed finished, marked in fact the supreme symbol of unswerving, selfless Love. It was a love that saw even those who placed him there, and I never forget my own share in that appalling crime, as sons of the same Father, each of them part of the Creator's purpose, each beloved, ordained, predestined. Each played a part in the incarnation and revelation of Love.

Three Days Ago
More talking in the evening, but the big event of the day was a ride with Marcus to a village near Jordan river where he was to settle an order for timber. It was on the way back that we dismounted in a grove of olives, hobbled the horses, and Marcus spoke again of Phoebe, his wife. "Paul, I would die for her," he said and he told me that she was losing weight and strength and appetite, and of his continued fear that death might claim her. "Come and see her, Paul," he said and took me to his home. She is so beautiful. Marcus told her we had spoken of their love for each other and the Christ in me spoke directly to her. Little by little she expressed a great gnawing fear of rejection, of inadequacy, of failure to conceive, and then of being scorned in a foreign land. She had jealousy to face, she said, from some of the older women for they taunted her, telling her that, if

she failed her husband, she would be given slave-status again. She might then be sold in the market place. She wept and Marcus held her close but could not comfort her. The Christ then spoke through me of the Father, Creator, the Love Who made her, Who had given her life and Who would never leave her, Whose Love reached her now through Marcus and Whose Love Marcus knew through her. Faith in that Love reached beyond the body, beyond the seas and skies and was the deep meaning of Life. Of all this the Christ in me spoke.

When I stopped we were silent again and Phoebe's tears had ceased. I stood and moved to the door, Marcus joined me and we left his house in silence together.

In the evening I spoke to them all of the Chosen People, of the Law and of Messiahship. They were surprised, interested, and puzzled, having never had a Jewish friend to share such things with them! (The idea of a Messiah appealed to them and the thought that each of them was called to be the World's Saviour, as Jesus had been called and I felt myself called as well.)

Two Days Ago
So much has happened. I feel history being made in some secret, sure way. I am very tired, My Lord's Words through my voice are spoken to me as well as to those who hear me. I spent the day on the hills alone.

"Tell us why you left Damascus and are in Pella and not with the followers of this Way in Jerusalem," they asked me as we met for food together in the evening. So I told them why there was fear and suspicion surrounding me and of my own uncertainty that I could ever persuade them that I knew Jesus, had seen him alive and was as much entitled to be called an apostle as those who had known him before his crucifixion. I told them that I saw the resurrected Jesus and the Christ, alive throughout the world and not merely, as in the tradition of Judaism, as the one Messiah who would prove the Jews to be chosen and beloved beyond all other nations. They nodded in agreement and seemed to understand this universal idea.

"But I am being prepared to return to Jerusalem," I concluded, "and your love and acceptance of me and your understanding of the Love that is the true Christ, is strengthening me for my return as only the Holy Spirit can do." And I knew Christ amongst us, blessing us richly.

Yesterday
The immensity of the power of Christ working in me overwhelms me as it also does those who are sharing this experience in Pella with me. I had told them last night of my baptism by Ananias in the Damascus river and that it signified for me the life-giving Spirit of Love that cleansed, freed, embraced and washed me in the Water of Life and Love in whose flood I would willingly be carried for evermore.

Today Marcus came to me and asked whether I would come down to the river below the town, to a deep pool not far from the ford I had crossed when I first reached Pella. Since the evening when Phoebe had wept and shared her fears, he said, she had been so different — full of life and happiness. "She seems to have been made whole again," he said. He wanted me to witness a symbolic descent into the water by Phoebe and him as a sign that they recognised the love they had for each other as truly given to them from their Creator, Love Itself, a stream from the Water of Life that flooded the universe. This, they said, they had learnt from me as I had shown it to them in the Love that reached me in Christ.

Of course, I went with them gladly. Children and a few women washing their clothes in the stream and two men watering camels at a trough watched us curiously. Marcus was well-known as a prosperous business man, son of a wealthy trader. I wonder what they thought! But in a Greek city the unusual is generally approved, where to Jews the unusual is generally suspect. As they came up out of the water, hand in hand, laughing, I heard Christ in my heart saying, 'Beloved children! I am pleased with you,' and Marcus called to me and I ran down to them, took Phoebe's other hand and we ran back up the hill together, Phoebe gasping, panting, hair dripping, and so home, with a rare joy.

Wine flowed freely that night, and I told them that soon I must leave them. Then I told them, as Ananias had told me, of Jesus' last meal with his friends and how he had spoken of his departure from the body as symbolised by wine, his blood poured out and bread, his body broken, and we drank a toast to my Lord and broke up a loaf and passed round the pieces and so shared him with them, and we knew that meetings and partings and life and death were all one in the life of the Spirit — and we ate and drank with joy and gaiety. Death was rich and vital to us as a movement to fuller life in Love and Love knows no parting or decay. In Christ death has no Dominion.

Today

I plan to move on from Pella. How wonderful these weeks have been and how, through them all, I have grown in faith in the Christ in us all and in Love Itself, God, Creator and Father, I have been neither teacher nor preacher here, but a sharer of Love and they have given to me the Christ in them as much as they have received the Christ from me.

This is where the Gospel I preach is unique. Jesus has revealed the Christ as God's Love given in us and each one of us is called to radiate this Love. Only the Christ Spirit can unite us to one another and make of us one spiritual body, a body with many members, as has the human body, made one by Love Who made us in His image and Who loves each individual He has made and made for His service.

One week later

I had not wanted to leave Pella. It had been a place of happy friendship. The power of the Spirit of Christ, the graciousness of my Lord Jesus, the Love shed among us, filled our hearts and made that place a milestone in my life. Yet, I was right to leave them. It would have been easy to stay and be deaf to my Lord's call, but the call was clear and I decided rather suddenly that I must go. I wondered, the night before I left, whether he was calling me to

cross Jordan and set my face towards Jerusalem.
Was I now ready? But I had no clear sign. When I
left, my steps, or were they Sheba's, turned me
south-east from the King's Highway and finally up
into these hills. Now I am here it seems right that I
should have a few quiet days to consolidate my
learning, of Love, of patience, of humility. Then I
will travel through Gilead to Jerash, the largest city
of the Decapolis and, unless my Lord has told me
otherwise, I may visit Ramoth-Gilead and if I am
called to Jerusalem I can cross the river and journey
via Jericho. But I have no clear plan. It will be
shown me daily what I should do.

It is a week since I left Pella and I am on the way to
Jerash. I have been camping with some herdsmen
high up the Wadi Yabis. They are living in rough
stone houses, moving from one place to another
every three or four days to fresh grazing for their
goats. It was strange to be speaking Aramaic again,
and they are rough but friendly people and offered
me food and shelter when I first met them. So, I am
pausing here, climbing, on foot or with Sheba, alone
during the day, up into the hills. At every chasm or
gorge I wonder whether I am by the brook Cherith
where Elijah stayed as I am doing. Every shepherd
and goatherd is versed in the legends and stories of
our people, and every village proudly claims that
they know a cave where Elijah slept or offers to show
me the birthplace of Elisha. This is the country, too,
of my own tribe of Benjamin and I feel, here, very
much part of my own tribal history and part of the
whole great unfolding of the history of my people,

the Chosen Ones. Am I, dare I, in the secrecy of this journal, wonder whether I am one of the great universal succession of prophets, preachers, leaders, called as they were by God to reveal His Truth?

I look back over my life and realise I have been given an amazingly wide range of opportunities and experiences. Why should God have equipped me, armed me, with such a wide spectrum of viewpoints, if He is not calling me to use them for His purpose? I feel as if I stand at the centre of His universe. Indeed, as I write these words, I can see in the distance a silver shimmer which is the Great Sea itself, uncharted waters that reach to the edge of the world. I realise that each of us is at the centre of His World; from His feet the World reaches in every direction to its furthest end and each of us is loved by his Creator, and called to pass that Love on to each of his fellow men. Is my calling, then, to lead the Israelites into a wider land of Promise, a Kingdom of Love embracing the whole world? I always felt bound and enclosed in Jerusalem. Temple worship has become inturned, ritual has become hardened, tradition is confused with truth and hierarchy with goodness. I am called by Love to freedom, to trust in, to serve, Love, as seen in Jesus Christ. I wish I had known him as a man.

I had paused then, thinking deeply and had suddenly, seemingly irrelevantly, remembered a young man of my age I had met in Damascus. He came from a wealthy family in Jerusalem and was a new young ruler of his synagogue. He had asked Jesus what he should do, and Jesus had told him to sell up and join him. This had hit him hard — too hard — for he was very rich and he had gone off. He had been so shocked after Jesus' death that he had done just that, sold everything and fled with the many others to Damascus and become a follower of the Way. He came back to my mind just then for I felt Jesus saying the same to me, 'What shall I do?', I was asking. 'Sell all you have for Love,' was the reply.

At that point was my heart full or breaking? Suddenly I was filled with energy and leapt on to Sheba and galloped up the hillside, shouting to heaven, " I will! I will!" Stone and gravel were flung by Sheba's pounding hooves and I grabbed my cloak as it flew off my shoulders and waved it, exulting, in the air. I was the latest, newest, wildest, surest of the prophets, proclaiming a new Jerusalem, a new world, the whole world a mighty army in the service of Jesus, under the Lordship of Love, our Father, Creator.

Sweating, panting, breathless, Sheba and I came back under the tree where I had left my possessions. I stripped and washed off the sweat in the stream and began feverishly to record this revelation. As I wrote, I saw again the dead body of my Lord on that cross and I was sobered and realised the price that must be paid if one is to serve Love truly, wholly, faithfully.

Later that evening one of the goatherds called me to eat with them and they chided me, laughing, for they had seen me gallop, shouting up the hillside. There was wild rough talk and sly glances for they thought I was caught up by lusty, sexual hungers. The love I know has no appeal to the world where pride and greed and lust and possessions hold sway. Yet at the heart of every human being is the longing to be loved and these rough men do not know they are loved by Love for ever. Full of these awesome thoughts I climbed early this morning, more soberly to the top of Mar Elyas, the hill overlooking Elijah's town of Tishbe. I called on Elijah and Elisha to give me their blessing, for indeed, my calling is as theirs, to be a prophet of God, a prophet of Love.

I am alone. The moon is full and the day has been hot, so the cool of evening has brought blessed relief. I huddle in my mantle under an old thorn bush in a rocky hollow looking down towards the Jordan valley. Unless this night brings a clear message I shall move on to Jerash tomorrow. Sheba crops the grass nearby and I have a thorn fire burning. My lamp flickers low and I feel these days of preparation are coming to an end.

Jerash

It was strange next day, to be travelling again amongst crowds and strangers; it was some months since I had done so. I joined the road from Pella to Jerash. It was full of travellers and traders. There were Nabateans journeying to Petra, camels en route back to the east having exchanged spices for cloth and pearls and gold for leather goods and skins. There were carts loaded with timber, black basalt, Egyptian granite and other building stone, and there was a cohort of Romans marching in formation. Soon I saw in the distance the roofs and pillars of the great city and though I had been told in Pella that I would be impressed by Jerash I was unprepared for what I found. It was clear as we passed through fields of grain and beans and orchards of olives and figs that the city was well sited in a wonderfully fertile valley, and its surrounding lands were well farmed and cared for. I arrived at the Northern entry and passed through the massive city walls. There were fruit, bread and water sellers at the gate and I gratefully bought figs and grapes and drank from a water trough kept full with water from Jerash's always flowing Golden River. There were stables near the gate and I left Sheba and walked first down the main street to a huge oval piazza, surrounded by pillars, at the south end. A city has been on this spot for centuries, each new conqueror adding to its splendour, but it is now a purely Hellenic city, with a colonnade of vast Ionic pillars and, to the

141

west, on a hilltop, a splendid temple to Artemis.

Tarsus, Antioch and Jerusalem have had developments over the years and destruction over centuries of history. Much, consequently, was unplanned and haphazard, though in Jerusalem the Herods have carried out impressive developments and building projects that have given it a marked stamp. But Jerash has a special beauty in its pure unchallenged Greek buildings.

The oval piazza is both meeting and market place, full of people trading or travelling or sitting round talking, and I moved from group to group listening and occasionally questioning. The Jewish quarter is on a hill outside the main town, but I decided I would try to find hospitality in the city, and finally succeeded in being offered a room with a Greek family. It is here, in his courtyard I am writing. The father is a potter who works in his house in the Cardo, the colonnaded main street and his sons sell his pots in the piazza. The beautiful older buildings here are as lovely they say, as in any Greek city and mercifully they survived the city's conquest under General Pompey a hundred years ago. Soon after settling in my room I strolled round the city. I found a well-used theatre, temples to many gods, and everywhere the great Ionic pillars forming colonnades and supporting roofs that gave cool shade to the side-walks and shops. So beautifully and smoothly paved are the streets that chariots drive down at break-neck speed, scattering pedestrians and even merchandise! The most unexpected thing for me was to find the place was a hive of development and activity. Clearly the Romans have plans to make this city one of the greatest tributes to their might. It is on the eastern edge of their Empire, commanding trade routes to the east across vast desert lands to unknown, unexplored countries, and then south by the old King's Highway to the heart of the Nabatean kingdom at Petra. Then, of course, it reaches westward to the coast of the Great Sea and northwards by the route I had roughly travelled from Damascus.

I roamed the streets this evening and my mind teemed. Here at the edge of the Empire the world, in every direction is open to me. 'Where, Lord? When?' I cried in my heart, and the Christ in me gave me no exact answer but a very sure awareness that my wanderings were not for ever and soon a direction would be clear. I wandered into the Temple of Zeus and knew that he was symbol for the Greeks of the supreme Father, God, with all the might of earthly power and heavenly strength, awesome, fearful, towering above all. Then towering above Zeus I saw Love, Father, God, above all earthly power and heavenly strength, above all, through all and in all, but brought close to us on earth by His uniquely beloved son, Jesus, Love incarnate, the Christ.

Then, in the temple of Dionysius I found a tribute to all earthly delights and joyful revelling in life, in the god of wine and dance and music, so suspect by Jews as leading to drunken orgies, sexual indulgence, licentiousness, permissiveness – Love dragged down to earth in self-love! "Oh, Jesus my Lord!" I almost shouted aloud, for I saw him hanging on the cross, among the vine leaves and wine cups of the Dionysiac ritual and feasting, and I rejoiced that I had died with him and knew in my resurrected life with him a joy and delight with which no earthly orgy or revel could compare, for he loved me and in that was my joy. His use of bread and wine symbolised with deep and real simplicity what a Bacchanalian feast failed to show.

Never before had I entered pagan temples with such

understanding. This was an experience forbidden to every Jew. I was dressed as a Greek and I felt no guilt or fear but understood anew and felt a great reverence in remembering that the Holy of Holies, in the Temple in Jerusalem, was empty, forbidden to man. There was held a mystery of great holiness, the Shekinah, that brooded as a cloud, a light, and spoke to the heart of man of the glory of God.

Here are also many smaller shrines and the last I visited, the most ancient of then all, was the temple of Artemis. A wide new stairway is being constructed, for it is high up on the hillside and it is clear that the ascent to the innermost part of the Temple is in itself to be impressive, symbolic of the climb of the soul from earth to heaven. This shrine, dedicated to the chaste Diana, spoke to me of the hunger of a man for the highest, the purity of forest and woodland, of wild creatures and all the natural world. I had often been told as a boy in Tarsus of the great temple built in her honour across the mountains in Ephesus − one of the wonders of the world, they said. If my journeys ever took me there I would remember Jerash and how its many and varied pagan beliefs in so many gods had shown me how, far above all their most lofty ideals, was the God of gods, Love and how its lowest, lustiest expressions were a pathetic longing to bring Love down into our daily lives, as Jesus my Lord had done with no temple other than his body in life.

Just before sunset a Roman cohort passed into the city through the South Gate, marching briskly like puppets under their general's command till he halted them and dismissed then to get food before going back to the barracks for the night. They told me they had come from Petra where they had been strengthening the garrison, supporting the Nabateans there against hill tribes and invaders who were plundering and stealing. As I watched them I thought of the military might of Rome and of her worldly power and authority, of the wisdom of Greek philosophy and logic and learning, and how foolish it all seemed when laid alongside the love of God in Jesus. Love makes nonsense of the wisdom of the so-called wise, of the educated and well-born. Everything in the world is transient but Love is unchanging, over-ruling and reveals all human power as foolishness. Before I returned to the potter's house I hired a boy to care for Sheba for the days until I again move on. I feel Jerash had much to teach me, though I feel also a strange hostility here. Is it the influence of paganism? Of the military power of Rome? Of my isolation from the Jewish community with whom I have made no contact? But these are first impressions. I must wait for the experience of the days.

It is three weeks since I last wrote my journal. Bewildering, difficult days. I am learning, in whatever state I am, to accept all experience as Love's gift, suffer it if need be and not let it go until it has revealed its meaning. Light cannot be richly experienced until it shines in darkness as the gentle silver moonlight shone in the darkness, comforting me in those first days after my accident. Life is cherished more dearly when bodily death seems near. Love is more precious in loneliness. I have known darkness, death and loneliness in these last days and my Lover has never left me however alone I felt.

In my last entry I wrote of my arrival in Jerash, of the impact this great city made on me and of the message I found in the pagan temples. I also mentioned the faintly hostile feeling I felt. I thought it was because I had met no Jews and had made no contact with the Jewish community which was, in fact, in the old city across the river among the trees. The atmosphere of the new town was created largely by the crowds of restless soldiers — cohorts, for the most part, from Syria. They were impatient with the tedium of being far from home. They were at the eastern edge of the Roman Empire with no thought of conquering new territory, for only vast stretches of desert lay to the east, crossed by old spice routes and tracks worn by pearl traders which converged on the city. To the south lay the road to Petra through the mountains of Moab. Only trained and experienced soldiers were delegated to go there and those left in Jerash were a surly lot, builders, artisans and stone-masons, untrained for war, unwilling conquerors, pining for home, army riff-raff with indifferent leadership and little discipline outside the barrack square. The building programme in Jerash would provide work for them there for years. I had misjudged them for I had expected friendship to a stranger who spoke fluent Greek and Asian Latin and approached them with courtesy, but they were haughty or sullen or both, and scornful when they knew I was a Jew.

It was several days after my arrival here, still unsuspecting of hostility from even the lowest of the conquerors to the conquered, I was watching the building of the new colonnade along the Cardo. A long-awaited load of timber had recently arrived from Lebanon. Its non-arrival had held up the work for several weeks beforehand. Great granite columns and some beautifully worked capitals and tracery lay about waiting scaffolding for their erection. Much sawing of timber was going on both for building and support and finished scaffolding was being hoisted into place alongside the cut and numbered stones that would be hauled into place next day. Soldiers were shouting instructions, nearly drowning the orders of the officer in charge. The boys of the town had gathered with interest, to watch techniques and team-work which the local people had never devised or needed, for the old Greek temples and buildings had been built too many years before and still stood firm. I, too, watched with interest.

It was mid-day and very hot and onlookers had dispersed for the afternoon's rest. Building was becoming a familiar sight to them while a new experience and novelty for me, at least on this vast scale. Two soldiers were hoisting one great trunk with ropes, levers and pulleys to two men on a platform of scaffolding above. I stepped forward to add my strength and help steady the swaying tree. They looked at me with surprise and the men above were hurling abuse in rough soldiers' Latin that I was not meant to, and indeed could only partly, understand. I was taken aback having had so many friends over the years in the Roman army.

Then the accident happened. I think one of the men above must have slipped. I saw his body in the air, heard shouts and saw the timber falling. Then I felt a great blow on the head, another on my thigh and knee, more shouting and then the thudding of feet which merged with a pounding in my head and then I must have lost consciousness. It cannot have been much later when I was aware of seemingly muffled voices, steady, dull, marching feet and then the order to halt. The pounding stopped and one pair of feet came closer and an army boot stabbed at my back.

"Lift the timber!" the commanding voice called. Feet came nearer and then I heard the command "Lift!" The weight moved off my leg and I felt only agonising throbbing in leg and head.

"Shoulder hoist!" I heard. "March!" Then — "That fellow is nearly dead. Leave him. His countrymen will collect the body." Their tramping began again and as the sound of the soldiers died away I tried to move one arm. I moved it to my head and felt what must have been blood congealing in my hair and down my face and neck. I dared not move my legs and, anyway, strength had gone again and my arm dropped.

Daylight was fading fast when I heard children's voices.

"Don't touch it! It's a man!"

"It's dead," called a younger voice, followed by childish screams and running feet that faded into the distance.

After they had gone I dreamed again my old dream of the battle of Light and darkness. I tried to move my leg but a shot of pain knocked me back into unconsciousness. It must have been dawn when the children were back again.

"Hey!" I heard. "Master, are you dead?" I stirred.

"He's alive!" I heard and again they ran away. No one in Jerash would know me, miss me or look for me. The man in whose house I had lodged would be puzzled. We had met little. The soldiers had their own casualty to attend to and had made it clear that I was of no concern to them. I felt desperately alone, cold, thirsty and in pain and soon unconsciousness drove out any further thought.

Some time later I heard slow, quiet footsteps drawing nearer. There was no sound other than a steady, quiet tread. Then I felt a touch on my face and

148

I opened my eyes. A young boy knelt by me. "Sir," he said, "can you drink it? You should. It is good for you. I saw your eyelids flicker." There was a pause between each sentence and his young, gentle voice brought soothing peace and calm to my pain. "I knew you were alive. Please try, Master. You need not die. I know," the boy went on, "because my father died but I gave him water and he got better." Another pause. "But in the end he died. Please drink, sir," and he put his young hand under my head and lifted it and I was able to move one arm and guide the vessel to my lips.

Then, as clearly as if I were in full consciousness I heard the words, "You are the Christ, child of the living God." Were they spoken to me or to the boy? They were true for each of us. My Lord was with us and Love spoke these words to us both. The Christ was in each of us, I, the receiver, the boy, the giver and the cup of cold water was the symbol of Love. I, also, was the giver and he the receiver of my love, and gratitude, for the service he had given to me for Love. Was my leg, I wondered, broken? My head was gashed and still bleeding. My body was dead but the Christ in me and the Christ in that boy were one and Love was healing us, each for the other.

"Master," the child said, "I'm going to look after you. Where do you live? Have you a home, a wife, a son? I will go and tell them you are hurt and they will come and fetch you."

"I am a stranger in Jerash," I muttered to the boy. He bent low to listen. "I am visiting here." My eyes closed.

"I'll be back soon," he said and I heard him run away. I slept and once or twice in the dark I found I could turn my body a little and thought that my leg, though badly crushed was not broken. The boy had left the vessel of water by me. I could just reach it and drank again. I slept but it was still dark when I woke again and drew my cloak more closely and found there was also a sheepskin over me. Had the boy returned and brought me that as well? I lay musing in the darkness. They were not idle moments for, yet again, my Lord Jesus, as in all the events that come to me, used them to illustrate the eternal care and control and devotion of his love. I seem to have moved in my thinking far beyond the structure and discipline of the Jewish Law. The Jews know of God's Love and strive, by their obedience to His Law, to be worthy. Jesus shows me that Love loves me, regardless of worth and that He loves all that He has made. How can we call what Love has created unworthy or unclean? Light grew and I realised it was the moon and saw some fruit by my side, olives and figs and could only say in my heart, "This is the Christ. These children have within them the Spirit of Love."

I dragged myself up slowly and bathed my head. It throbbed and stabbed and I felt a deep, jagged wound but that would heal. I found I could move my leg enough to drag myself along. The leg was not broken but I dared not straighten it and lay back and thought, as long and hard as a throbbing head allowed, about the body. How easily its needs and appetites take us over, demanding our care and loving attention. With throbs and aches and hungers and lusts it drags us down to serve and satisfy it and how quickly we stifle our souls to serve this lesser and lowest of gods, giving all our love of self to its service. Then I saw him again, my Lord and lover, his body hanging lifeless on the cross, dead, and I knew him at my side, living and loving. I knew that my body, whether broken or bruised was merely a temple − like the pagan temples

I had so marvelled at some days before — of the Christ, the Spirit of Love, eternal and in me for ever.

Now, this I set down, in awe and wonder. (How could I have thought so clearly when so close to unconsciousness?) My body died to me. I felt no pain. My mind was clear, my heart on fire with love for my Lord and — my leg obeyed my command to stand. Oh, yes, I tottered a bit. Like a new-born lamb at birth, I fell, but only briefly. I stood, supporting myself against one of the newly-erected Ionian pillars of the colonnade. Dawn was breaking. I looked down at my crumpled, blood-stained cloak, the sheepskin, the water-pot, the remains of figs and olives. Had these gifts been only in the service of the body? No, that boy had, through them, given me love; the Christ in him had met the Christ in me and the gifts for my bodily needs were symbols of Love given and received. How else can we show Love, Whom we worship, other than in service to each other? How acknowledge our kinship as children of one Father except as Jesus did when he demonstrated by his lifeless body on the cross that his spirit was liberated to love, Christ resurrected to all eternity?

So I stood, propped against the pillar, as the new day dawned and knew my physical body had no longer life of its own. I had nailed it to the cross that the Christ might be raised in me. Then, before these thoughts were formed I heard running feet again and children's voices coming close and they were back again. One of the boys came closer and said, "Oh, Master, are you all right? Did you find the fruit? Are you better? We have come to get you to a shelter we know. These soldiers are rough men and might treat you badly. I brought my friends to help me get you there. We thought we would have to carry you. Can you walk?"

"Was it you," I asked, "who brought the water last night and later the fruit and the sheepskin?"

"Yes, I brought them," said the boy. "You said you had no family here so we decided to be a family for you. That's why we're here now."

They gathered my things together and a little girl with them took the water-pot and they helped me hobble away from the building site to a place, half cave, half house, lined with stone and with a stone portico. It had, at some time, been a home until the Romans came and set their building programme in notion, and it had been then too close for safety. It was empty and clean and had a stone shelf along one side with an oven underneath – a typical, simple, Arab home, obviously abandoned and unused.

"We often come and play here," said another of the boys. "No one will bother you and we will bring you food and water."

I was a great discovery for them and they made me part of their world of play and fantasy. A week passed with frequent visits from them and, with their care, I gathered strength, limping for several more days, but each day going a little further and my head wound healing fast. They came and went faithfully. Simeon, the boy who had first befriended me, was the most faithful and tireless. He retrieved my goods, my wallet and scrip and this journal and my papers and weaving gear that I had left with the potter at the North Gate, wrapped in a cloth. I was glad to find it intact. The potter had kept it safely and had wondered why I had not returned. The news of the soldiers' accident had reached him but he had not associated me with that. Even my money was safely inside. I had paid for a weeks' stabling for Sheba and Simeon went to find her, found her well, and paid the stable-boy for the coming days. I loved that boy dearly and his care for me brought a warmth and peace that was healing and exhilarating to my spirit. It was untainted by physical desire and the healing of my body followed naturally on the wholeness of the Christ in me. My body obeyed the Christ who lived and moved in love between us and I soon walked, ran, jumped and the children and Simeon laughed. "We did it!" they called. "We made you better! We stopped you dying!"

"Yes," I said. "You have brought me to life! We will meet tonight. Bring some bread and fruit and I will give you a feast in my house, for soon I must leave you and go on my way."

"Oh!" They said. "Must you go?"

"Yes, I have work to do," I replied, "but you will remember me for ever and I will always remember what God has given to me in these days of your caring for me."

They were Jewish children, I had discovered, from Syria, their homes being in the Jewish settlement across the Golden River. They came over daily to mix in the city life, to run errands or trade in the oval piazza or along the Cardo, that splendid and busy colonnaded street that stretched from the piazza to the North Gate which I had explored on my first evening, now more than a month ago.

When our feast was over that evening and the children had gone home, Simeon stayed for the night and we sat under the stars and I told him of my Lord Jesus. He nodded his head often in agreement. "I know," he said from time to time and when he said nothing I knew we were travelling together in the Spirit and the Christ in each of us was one.

The feast with the children had been joyful and cheerful. I had brought wine and cheese and bread, grapes and dates and some Greek sweetmeats from the market and I remembered how Ananias had told me of Jesus' last meal before he left them. So we celebrated our delight in each other by sharing a loaf, breaking it and handing pieces round. Then we passed round the vessel in which Simeon had first brought me water and this time I mixed it with the wine. "This is my body which you healed," I said, as I broke off bread and gave it to them. "Remember the Love we share," and "This is my life-blood that you saved," I said, holding the cup. "Remember always that it is Love that gives us our life."

Then I said, "Gather round and I will tell you a story, a true story of a friend of mine," and I told them of my Lord Jesus and how he was the Messiah and was with me. They were fascinated, interested and puzzled, for they had had the synagogue teaching about Messiah and I realised how little I knew of Jesus' earthly life. It was hard to tell others about him without at least some detail of where and how he lived and what he had said and done. The children needed this and at one point they shuddered and thought I was speaking of a ghost − a confusion of disembodied spirit and spirit-wrapped body − for their teaching had told them of the spirits of the dead in Sheol. So I told them of his coming to me on the Damascus road and they were happy again and their eyes sparkled with recognition and understanding and I knew that they knew and understood the life of the spirit and the reality of God as Love and that Jesus, the Christ, was speaking to me and in me.

It is three days now since the children's feast. I plan to leave Jerash tomorrow on the King's Highway and travel towards Philadelphia. I have wandered again and again around this ancient and beautiful city and realise what a transformation these new developments by the Romans are bringing, not just to Jerash, but the whole world. Already they have started here a new piazza, new hippodrome and theatre, linked together by new beautifully laid-out roads with gateways into the city. Walls and colonnades are being strengthened, old temples enlarged and restored and plans made for new ones. They are all in their early stages and will take many years to complete. Where shall I be when it is finished? For I feel sure my Lord will not bring me this way again.

Several times the children have come and said, "Tell us again about your Lord Jesus," and I tell them that they can know him themselves and learn from him, just as he has shown me, of Love, our Father God, Who is with us and in us and cannot be held by any walls. God above all those lesser gods of the temples of Jerash. "In the way you care for each other, friends, strangers or even enemies, you will meet and know him," I said, "and his love will keep on growing more and more as your bodies grow, and your lives will be filled with qualities that only Love in the Spirit of Jesus can reveal in you."

They clapped their hands and Simeon looked at me with wonder. One morning they took me over the Golden River to their homes in the Jewish community and I met their families. I knew my time in Jerash was coming to an end so I merely accepted their natural hospitality to strangers – fruit and bread and cheese and wine – and returned to my 'home' in the city. I have been practising telling of Love through Jesus the Christ to these children! Soon, surely, I will have the faith to speak boldly to my own people and tell them with confidence that Messiah has come.

Only what I know for myself and from my own

experience can be recognised as true in words. All that is imitated or copied or second-hand is sham and children are quick to recognise this. Sadly, strangely, I see the Law itself, though given by God to Moses, as second-hand. It is an illustration, a stage on the journey of the People of Israel, relevant for a time, a school-master to lead us to Christ. The Law tells us to obey blindly. Now I see through a glass, darkly, but I am moving to the place where I shall see Love clearly, face to face. Children know instantly when we are true and trustworthy and I, who feel there is in me the potential gift of preacher, learnt from them. They so quickly recognise the twists and deceits by which we feed or disguise or blind ourselves to our self-love. Only by giving up, by denying the demands of the mortal body, so richly symbolised by Jesus on the cross, can the Love within us, be truly liberated in the service of Love's beloved children, made in His Image. This one thing I know, as I die to self and live for Him, in daily, hourly contact with Him, so the Christ lives in me.

Pisgah

Jerash is behind me. I am on the road to Philadelphia. I have stopped at a caravanserai, at a junction where the King's Highway continues south by the Nabatean road to Petra and a trade route turns off to the east to Baghdad. I am tempted to go to Petra. People speak of the wonders of this ancient city carved in the rose and gold rock and carrying fold on fold of rainbow-coloured seams of strange beauty. But I am no traveller after wonders, no trader in expensive merchandise. I carry at my heart the great wonders and ever-growing mysteries of Love and my goods to bestow are treasures beyond price. If I go to Petra it will be because the Christ within directs me and not because I am looking for new experiences or wealth to adorn my self-esteem. I am beloved of Love and need no more. My experience with the Jerash children and their eagerness and understanding of Love, has given me a great hunger for more knowledge of Jesus' life in Galilee and Judaea for, though this will always be, for me, second-hand and, in a sense, irrelevant to my knowledge, it is illustrative material, confirming experience. Experiences of his earthly life are the riches of the followers who lived alongside him before they understood that he was Messiah and that the Holy Spirit of Love was in them also.

What a hub of the universe a place like this is! There are cooking fires in every corner and every-

157

where the smell of roasting meat and oil, the smoke of thorn fires, the fresh dung of animals. Loads of merchandise are dumped and piled within the walls, smelling often of spices and incense.

Some fires are even burning incense, thrown on in odd handfuls to add another scent to the whole. Men are squatting in ones or twos or small groups, some close to their wares, some chewing cane or nuts or smoking pipes. Camels and asses are being loaded or off-loaded and, with grunts and brays and shouts, a party will move off and very soon another will arrive. It is crowded and amongst them all I am alone with my Lord. I talk to anyone who will listen but can contribute little to talk of profit and loss, of thieves and brigands, or women and their ways, so, in a dim corner, with Sheba safely hobbled and fed, I write a brief entry.

Faces are lighted by fires, lamps and flares. In the eyes of these people I see fear and greed. They cling to their friends and possessions or snatch their food. They are unsure of each other; the world is an enemy and they are armed against it. The banter of laughter or casual talk, the whispered mutterings and gesticulations, all with a background of animal groans and grunts, speak to me of unsatisfied longings. The world is gathered here, There are traders and travellers from across seas and deserts, citizens and nomads, crossing each others' lives briefly. Each is beloved of Love, made in Love's image, longing to be accepted as the child of one Father but they do not know this and do not know for what they hunger. They are starved for the love my Lord Jesus has shown to me and that he showed to every man during his earthly life when he lived in love with mankind. I am ashamed that I still feel some envy of his friends who daily lived so close to him.

My return over Jordan is near. I know it with a sure knowledge beyond my own desires. I will direct my will, even if against my will, so that it flows unresisting in the stream of Love's will. I am restless. I am tired of casual meetings and partings, though many have I known in Arabia in a love, rich and eternal — Ananias and Judas, Timothy, Marcus and Phoebe, Simeon and many others. Am I never to see then again?

Fitfully I sleep. Many round me sleep also. There is no deep silence but always restless tossings, grunts or movement. How can Love touch these starving folk? How did my Lord on earth ever reach them? I remember how I had been told that crowds had flocked to him. I remember Stephen's devotion. I remember my own jealousy and my own insatiable hunger for the love they knew. I realise, now that I know him, that he must always have revealed the nature of Love but he would never have forced Love on anyone or have tried to be seen as a god. Freely he gave all he had and humbly, a servant, he walked through life, through crucifixion, in obedience to his Father. Oh if these people, breathing heavily around me, could know him as I do, they would fall on their knees in this stinking, airless place of sweating bodies and openly proclaim God as Love and Jesus as Lord. We would all be caught in the glory of our Father, no more dimly lighted by lamp or flame but, in a blaze of Love, brighter than day, we would recognise each other as brothers.

Then my Lord spoke to me.

The message I received was not in words as when He first called me to him. The message was clear but had no human origin. It was the advice of no man, neither was it the outcome of my own thinking, nor the outcome of wants or wishes of my own. I was directed as Christ revealed it to me.

The time has come. I am to return to Jerusalem and claim my place among the followers of Jesus and learn of his earthly life through them. I am to make my Lord's name known among the Gentiles. My fear has gone, cast out by Love, and I am ready to preach and teach the love of the Christ which passes all understanding to all who come my way. There is a strange awareness in the message, too, that tempers the joy and certainty with which I now know my direction. I have come so close to and learnt so much of my lover and brother as we have journeyed together through the towns of the Decapolis and I can hear, though not in words, 'You will have much to bear for my name's sake, tribulations and suffering and I will bear all things with you for in Christ we are one.' An awesome, exhilarating sobering message, stored in my heart.

I write this at dawn and many are already on the move and some, I realise, must have left earlier and I will turn away to-day from the highway to Philadelphia. I will not, therefore, as I had thought I might, follow the King's Highway, through Nabatea, to that magical city of Petra, whose glory is spoken of by so many. I shall leave this hostelry and turn aside for one more day and night in the mountains, alone with my Love, to be reassured of his nearness. Then I will cross Jordan river and travel steadfastly to Jerusalem.

Quickly after writing the above I packed my things, saddled Sheba and left the hostelry. Can it have been so short a time ago? Just yesterday morning? I left the King's Highway and journeyed westward by hill tracks and wadis through Moab towards Mount Nebo. I had only travelled for an hour or so when two men on camels caught up with me, travelling home from Philadelphia to the Arnon River. We stopped together for food at Myin Musa where there was also plentiful water. Small boys brought us apricots and almonds and goats' cheese and we tethered our animals to the oak trees and rested. We were told by a shepherd that this was the spring from which the water first gushed out when Moses smote the rock when our people were dying of thirst on their journey to Canaan. Manahem, one of the two who had joined me, laughed. "There are many such!" He said and I thought there might well have been many, for Moses led a motley crowd. Many times must they have been thirsty, hungry, rebellious and Moses may well have struck many rocks, many times, if this sign was necessary to keep the masses together and give them strength to go further.

As the mid-day heat passed we set off again. After crossing the desert plateau we continued westward to a hilly region where sometimes the track wound down a wadi and we were amongst thick vegetation, where there were apricot and peach trees with oleanders and flowers in profusion. Sometimes we crossed a stream to follow the track up the opposite slope and back up the hillside. We rounded a shoulder where folds of the hills made us have to dip and then climb again, yet we were steadily, all the time, climbing higher until finally we were in the Mount Nebo region. Reaching a summit we saw to the left of us another peak and further ahead a mountain, which my companions told me was Mount Pisgah itself. The sun was setting fast and we decided we must camp for the night. We had seen tracks of lion and jackal and knew that it would be wise to kindle our fire, hobble the camels nearby and settle them and Sheba before darkness fell. This we did. Manahem had bread, dates and olives in his saddle-bag and I had goats' cheese and lentils which were soon boiling over the fire. The sun set and darkness fell. A nearly full moon rose and the land fell silent around us, save for the call of an animal or an owl's screech.

"Tell us more, Brother Paul," Azariah said, "of this man you say you met on the Damascus road." As we had journeyed I had told him of my friend and that I had journeyed from Damascus and was soon to return to Jerusalem.

"Gladly," I replied, and then, again, heard myself telling the story, not only of my meeting with Jesus but of his life in Galilee, his crucifixion in Jerusalem, his followers and my hostility to them all and then, of my meeting him alive, though I had seen his dead body on the cross and how I had grown so close to him in my months in Arabia that he was with me always, a live, sure, indwelling spirit. As each day passes my story grows richer and fuller and yet simpler and surer, for in each day's meeting with Jesus our closeness is more deeply revealed. Yet it is hard to pass on to others this awareness that we are so close that I can say that he, the Christ, lives in me. This is the message that I must pass on, for it is true for everyman throughout the world. There is in Christ neither Jew nor Nabatean, Greek nor Roman, bond nor free, male nor female. All are one through Jesus, the first to reveal the Christ to the world, the great lover of every one of us.

I told these two camel-drivers my story in greater detail. I told them why I had left Damascus and how I had been surrounded by distrust and suspicion amongst the Jews there. As I told my story I realised that the Damascus followers of the Way, even they, witnesses with me that he was alive, could not reach beyond their deep-seated conviction that the Chosen People were the Jews and that Jesus was Messiah for them alone. As I told my story I realised how far I had travelled since those Damascus days. That fiery and fearful Saul, who had so recently and mercilessly hounded them to prison had suddenly proclaimed triumphantly and confidently the resurrected Christ. No wonder they rejected me! I was insensitive and assertive. I had been so sure I was accepted by my lover that I had felt sure of their acceptance of me as well. How differently I would tell them now if I returned to them!

"Why are you not going back to Damascus?" Azariah asked. Why did I find the answer difficult?

"I am returning to Jerusalem," I replied, "because I am one of those who know Jesus and I want to learn from those who lived close to him during his life on earth, of what he said and did. I won't stay there long if they find me hard to accept as did his followers in Damascus."

"But we can tell that you are a scholar, a learned and intelligent man," Azariah said, "and you speak firmly and with conviction. We would love to have such firm certainty. But how, travelling as we do, on the edges of towns and villages, can we follow your way? We neither know, nor feel much need to know all this scholarly stuff about laws and behaviour. It is an easy life for those Jews who live near the Temple and are within reach of teachers and the synagogue."

"Yes," said Manahem, "we accept a Power behind the moon and the stars but, for us, every moment of the day must be given to the business of living."

"Do you remember yesterday," I replied, "when we drank from Moses' spring in the rock? Do you remember we noticed an ancient olive tree and noticed how new branches had been skilfully grafted to the old stock and branches from the old cultivated tree had been pruned away? We commented on the good husbandry. Remember? The old tree is like the old Israel which had been fruitful for many years. But you, like new branches can be grafted to the old stock and bring new life, new growth, new fruit to the old tree. Nourishment comes to you from the old roots. The roots feed you; it is not you supporting the roots, though the life and growth is yours. So, Jesus has brought new life, new truth, a new way for me. I know, through him, that Messiah has come; not as one man to redeem the world but so that every one of us may know himself to be messiah for his neighbour. The Christ is in each of us, reaching out to everyman, as Jesus did to me on my way to Damascus, giving such love to me that I know, for ever more, that Love is the Heart of God, spilling over in abundance on us all."

We were silent. Manahem had drawn his cloak round him and fallen asleep. Azariah smiled across at me, his eyes silvered by the moon and reddened by the firelight, then he, too, rolled over to sleep.

The moon had risen. I watched a desert beetle in the moonlight, burrowing out of sight. The sand trickled into the hole that it had made and I realised that each grain of sand that fell altered the shape of the desert. I felt that if I turned my thoughts to words they would fall like those grains of sand and make a movement that would change the shape of the world. Yet it is life, I mused, not words, that change the world.

I sat for a long time. "I have chosen you, my love," I heard, "but not you alone. I choose all created beings and love them all. But you, brother and lover, are to carry Love across, not just deserts, but oceans, not just in deep wadis but across mountain heights. To Moses I gave the vision of the Promised Land from this mountain. From this mountain you, too, will view, not just a Land of Promise for the few but a World of Love for the many. Moses never saw the actualising of his vision. Neither will you. But the roots planted by Moses are the roots of your inheritance. You, Brother Paul, are the new olive grafted on to the old tree and through you and by my power, the truth of Love will spread beyond the world you know, beyond your wildest dreams, into a world known only to the Father, the Creator, Love, and reached only through loving."

Strangely, strangely, under the moon, what the day had revealed came close and became understandable to me, so that, at last, I, too, drew my blanket close and fell back and slept. In that wordless world of dreams, in a union with Christ, my Lord, uniquely individual, yet widening into a unity of all Love's children, I saw a community that embraced the world, a consummation of love until, on some Last Day, all would be one through Love, revealed by Jesus.

I awoke with a start! Had I ever been asleep? The moonlight streamed across us and Mount Nebo was silhouetted against the blue-black sky. I got to my feet. A camel shuffled and breathed out a heavy groan. I drew my cloak close and stealthily moved away and up through trees and thorns on to the clear hillside. I climbed fearlessly, standing often to listen to the night. Sometimes there was just silence. Occasionally there was the sharp yelp of jackal or a nearby skirmish, a coney perhaps, but mostly I heard the inner heart-beat of the universe and a voice that said, "You, Paul, my beloved brother!" No more. Just repeated assurance that I was loved and free to love fearlessly in return, unchangeably and forever accepted, whole. I was transfigured as the moon is transfigured by the sun.

I reached a summit close to the peak and there I stood silent and time stood silent and still with me. A journey was ended and another was beginning. I knew a creative dying with Christ that brought to birth a new existence in the spirit, even under the conditions of this life, not conditions imposed by law but the conditions of the Love by Whom the universe was made. Every moment, every past experience of my life was woven into this new man, Paul, called to go, not just to that small world across the deep rift of Jordan river below in the moonlight, not just into that Promised Land that God had shown to Moses from the spot where I was standing but into the wider world, across the Great Sea, beyond and into as yet untrodden ways, beyond the might of Rome, beyond the wisdom of the Greeks, beyond the heights and depths of human dreams, into centuries unborn and then beyond time. In faith and hope and in Love I was to live as never before, not to form a cult, or any small selected group of like-minded thinkers, nor to band together followers of some life-style dictated by law or rite or ritual, but to free every individual brought to birth, bond or free, male or female, Jew or Gentile, to accept themselves as beloved of God, as I knew myself to be, through Jesus, my Lord. Then, in a service that is perfect freedom they may bring their own gifts to a world family, fathered by Love and, in the subjection of the mortal body, reveal the resurrection of the Holy Spirit of Love Itself.

The moon quietly sailed across the sky and faded as, from the same spot on Pisgah where Moses had stood, I saw, in the dim light near dawn, the land of Gilead, across all the land of Judah to the Great Sea. I saw Jericho, 'city of palm trees', below across the river. I saw far off, hazy in the early mist, the pinnacles of Jerusalem and the land lay silent as it had been before each dawn since God first made the garden of Eden for His children. Moses had seen into the future as I was doing. He died to the mortal body as, metaphorically, I die, also. From here, into the future, I was to set out.

For a long time I stayed there on Mount Nebo, at one with all creation. I moved from Chaos and Darkness to Order and Light. I moved from the beginning of time when the heaving crust of the universe folded the mountains and valleys, from desert to fertile land, from the snows of Hermon to the fruits of the farmlands. I moved through the mind of mankind from Osiris to Zeus, and to the gods of Babylon and Assyria; I sang Akhnaton's hymn to the Sun, the Moon and the stars as the Israelites did in captivity; I travelled through history with the patriarchs of my own people; I heard the calls of the prophets and knew the battles and struggles of our kings. I knew depths and heights and then came a deep stillness and a peace, beyond all understanding. At the heart of all things was Love, God of gods, Light of lights, Creator of our teeming universe, and Love saw all that was made and 'Behold, it was very good.' In the silence of the universe I, at its centre, was still, at peace, at the heart of Love.

For how much time I was caught in that silence I cannot tell. How close Moses was to me. He, the great leader, the Law giver, in the light of the burning bush on Sinai had come close to his God as I had outside Damascus. He had thrashed out a Law for the unruly mob he led and his life-work was fulfilled on this spot on Mount Pisgah where I now stood. "You will not go over Jordan," God had told him. "Your work is done." Here, where I stood, his earthly work was finished and mine began. He had given the Law. I was to give a Love that fulfilled and passed beyond the Law. His work ended, here, over-looking Jordan; mine was to begin here. Moses' Law was for the Jews, chosen, beloved people. The Love I knew, fulfilling the Law, was for every man alive, each one, chosen, beloved, each bringing unique gifts to the world.

I picked up two broken sticks at my feet as I mused and held them in my hands in the shape of the cross of his crucifixion and pledged myself to die daily, to be resurrected moment by moment in the Spirit of my Lord, in the Spirit of the Love by which he had lived.

Was it possible that dawn was already breaking behind me? I turned, and the horizon was palest apricot, gently turning to peach and gold. As the sun rose, so would I, now, in this new day, pass over Jordan to Jerusalem. I would travel to Antioch, Cyprus, Asia, Greece, maybe even to Rome. Lovers of Love, knowing the Christ in each other, would gather together from throughout the world, throughout all ages until a last day would come. Then with angels and archangels and all the company of heaven and earth, Jesus would be beloved, worshipped, King over all, with the Holy Spirit of the Christ in us. In Love, the Godhead, we should be made One as he and his Father are One. The day broke and tears of longing for the fulfilment of this Truth streamed down my face as I turned back to the camp. I wanted to be back before the sun had fully risen. The men would go down the King's Highway to Petra without me. Petra, I had known, was a great crossroad of the highways of the world and I had thought perhaps I would find there a new faith and confidence in my Lord's love that would give me courage to speak boldly there in his name. Yet, once more, this was not to be. I ran, stumbling but sure, in the dawn light towards our camp. Then, to my astonishment, as I ran, a strange and totally different unfolding of the way was revealed to me. Again, the words, "Not yet!" Was I to be once more turned from my path? After such sure direction I could not believe I heard aright! Then, clearly, suddenly, all fell into place! "To Jerusalem! Yes! But first to Damascus!" I was unlikely again to be east of Jordan and I was to see once more Ananias, Judas,

Jesus' friends who had fled from Jerusalem and from whom I had fled. I would share with them what I had learnt in these months away and all that I had seen so clearly in the night just past! Surely now, when they met the new Paul, Paul who had died to the body and risen in spirit, their fear and suspicion of me would fall away and I would then cross Jordan and return to Jerusalem by the route I had first intended with the knowledge that I was accepted by the brethren in Damascus and loved in Christ Jesus. I have learnt so much in the two years and more since I was with them and long to see them again and we will be able to strengthen and support each other and know ourselves the first-born of many brethren.

Last night the summit of Mount Pisgah was the summit of my dreams. All things have worked together for my Lord's will to be clear to me even to the chance meeting with Manahem and Azariah and even our chance conversation on the road which had seemed at the time trivial and irrelevant and has now been woven into my days.

We had been tethering the animals at our first stopping place. I had not previously mentioned to them that I would be parting with my horse either just before or when I reached Jerusalem for I would have no further need of her. "I could wish," Manahem said, "that you were returning to Damascus instead of having come from there, for I would have paid a good price for your horse and offered you my camel for your journey back. She belongs to my cousin in Damascus and at some time I must return the animal to him. It would have made returning her easier." We had laughed and spoken of other things.

There had been also the strange spirit-filled way I had heard myself speak of the grafting of the young olive on the old stock which had grown out of our chance observation of the olive tree at our side. I was the new olive, grafted on to the old Law and bringing new life to the tree. Then, last night, as Moses on Pisgah looked towards the Promised Land which he would never enter, so I knew that I would never embrace the whole world, as I longed to do, with the Love that I was destined to reveal.

It was as clear to me as the new light of day dawning round me. I knew I was not to cross Jordan by the ford below me as the Chosen People had done, but, leaving what I can only call 'the old man', my 'lesser self', there on the mountain I was to go, with all speed, by the fastest route to Damascus. Then, when it is clear that the purpose of that visit is fulfilled, I will, with little delay make for Jerusalem. I have found the confidence I had lacked and now know I can do all things through Christ who strengthens me.

Things happened quickly when I reached the camp. Manahem was delighted that I would return the camel to his cousin who, it turned out, lived at the other end of Straight Street. He gave me a good price for Sheba and I was glad of a camel that would travel at a steady speed and at a more even pace and so more quickly than a horse needing rest and water.

We were soon packed up and the men went off, Manahem on Sheba and Azariah on the second camel, to join the King's Highway for Petra. I have decided to spend the rest of this day in an oak grove nearby to write this journal. I will stay one more night before going back to rejoin the track close to the river that will finally lead me to the Damascus road. There is so much that it is important to recall and remember and I need a day alone before I face this great Future, this clear calling, to offer to all who come my way the love I know in Jesus Christ my Lord.

Damascus Again

It is now ten days since I left Pisgah. I am back in Damascus with Brother Ananias. To-day I am on the roof of his house under a palm branch thatch. The brethren have gone to a synagogue meeting and I am left to write up my journal. They will tell the gathering of my return and I will join them in the Sabbath worship tomorrow and then for the Love-feast the brethren share together afterwards. I look forward with joy to meeting them for I have so much to share, so much to hear and I long, after all these months, to meet with fellow lovers of my Lord.

After a last night in the grove on Mount Nebo when I slept soundly, I completed my journal, packed up my scrip and wallet and, knowing my wanderings and uncertainties were over I mounted, raised the camel and set off, leaving the Jericho crossing, passing travellers journeying that way to Judaea and travelled with good, steady speed towards Damascus. I was unlikely ever again to be east of Jordan and I looked forward with joy to my arrival. It felt as if the first stage of my life-journey was over and my life-work had begun. I longed to see Judas, Ananias and the other lovers of Jesus there; I longed to see whether all I had learnt in these wandering months was now accepted and I was at one with Jesus' friends. Were they still in love together? Still firm in their faith? Would their vision be one with mine? Would the cross of Christ mean to them all it meant to me? I needed their understanding and support.

I think that camel knew her way home for she went at speed by the road alongside the river, on to the road that passes under Mount Hermon and in four days we came to the wadi of my revelation where my lover had met me and revealed to me his love. It was mid-day and, in burning heat, a lonely, empty place. How could it look so dry and ordinary, with only a few trees down by the now dried up stream? Yet heaven and earth had been one for me there some two years or more ago! The earth was bare and barren but heaven had visited that spot and the place was holy.

On – to Damascus! When I was only a few hours away I had caught up with a group of traders travelling, also by camel, with silks, copper, pearls, perfume, gold and other Eastern merchandise. None of us knew the road for I had seen nothing when I last passed that way, so when we saw the city walls ahead of us we shouted for joy and urged our camels forward with their ungainly gait and arrived well before sunset. I went at once to Ananias' house and his surprise and delight were wonderful. His servants took the camel and he led me into the inner room, called for water and washed my feet, and gave me fresh sandals and dressed me in his best robe. Then, in the courtyard, in the shade of his flame-tree, in love and joy and peace, we exchanged the news of all that had happened since our last meeting. We drank wine and ate bread and fruit together and knew the Christ-spirit that bound us in such sure friendship.

The Nazarenes, as the refugee lovers of Jesus seem now often to be called, are flourishing in Damascus and from time to time they are joined by others from Jerusalem where Temple authorities are still trying to suppress them. "But, Saul," Ananias said, "there is no doubt that Jesus is the Messiah and, as our resurrected Lord, is establishing his Kingdom of Love amongst us." I longed to share with him my new found realisation of the Christ within us all, throughout the world, but it is important just now that I learn of Jesus, the Messiah, as they know him, risen amongst them, here and now. "You will meet two of the brethren from Jerusalem this evening," he said, "for they are staying here, a Cypriot and his young nephew, en route for Syria to sail from Antioch to Cyprus. The older man Barnabas, is wealthy and is selling land there to raise money for the poor brethren in Jerusalem. He is a strong follower of the Way. They are now visiting brethren in the town to say goodbye for they leave before dawn tomorrow. I am glad you will see them before they go. I believe they are both destined to be powerful messengers of Jesus, Messiah."

Just before sunset I took Manahem's camel to his cousin's house at the end of Straight Street. He was a pleasant man and surprised and pleased to have his animal returned to him so easily and so soon. He had heard, he said, of the Nazarenes but did not know any of them or much about them though he had heard that they met, sometimes, in the house of the apothecary, at the end of his street. "A friend of mine," I said. On the way back I called on Judas. He was not in his home so I left a message to say I was back and returned to Ananias.

A crowd had gathered when I got back and amongst them was the Cypriot of whom Ananias had spoken who had returned with John Mark, his

175

young nephew. Then followed a very blessed and valuable evening. Barnabas, the Cypriot, was a Jew who had been staying in Jerusalem with his sister, mother of the young Mark. Mark had actually known Jesus and often spoken to him. He had not been a follower as his father had recently died and he had had to stay at home to care for his mother but Jesus had often been to their house. I was fascinated by the boy. He had hung on Jesus' words and worshipped the man. He had tried hard to be one of the group closest to him but was so much younger than the rest and was needed so often at home that he was discouraged by them. He felt they did not want him, though Jesus had always welcomed him warmly. "But I listened to him often," he said, "and watched all he did and I was nearly captured by the guard when he was arrested but I wriggled away and later I went to see what happened and saw him crucified."

"I saw his dead body on the cross," I told the young man.

"But I was the first to see him alive after," young Mark replied. " I went in the dark and found the tomb empty and then I saw him and I told my mother and her friends when they came to embalm him. They were frightened of me and didn't recognise me in the half-light so I ran away to tell the others as I thought women would never believe me."

"I have seen him alive, too," I said to Mark. He looked at me uncertainly, disbelieving, for he had never seen me before.

Barnabas, I learnt from Mark, had only been a few months in Jerusalem on a visit. He had been immensely impressed by the Nazarene community and attracted by their open, fearless confidence and devotion, though he had been shocked by stories of persecutions they had undergone from the Temple authorities. I had no opportunity to tell him, though I longed to do so, of my own involvement in that. I was intent in drawing out from the young Mark all he had to tell of my Lord and only made casual contact with the others there. I was drawn to that young man and felt the old physical intensity I knew so well and he was drawn to me. I can nearly always handle that hunger now though the attraction is real. I no longer clamour for gratification for I need no other love than that which I receive daily from my Lord. The young John Mark told me that he was collecting sayings of Jesus and recording episodes from his life; in fact, he was writing a journal not unlike mine, of the stories remembered from the days before Jesus' crucifixion. He made me eager to return to Jerusalem to hear for myself these things.

"There are many, many more than I have collected," Mark said. I was ready to tell him of my meeting with my Lord when we were interrupted by a servant to fill our wine cups and then Mark was joined by two friends and a chance of further talking together never returned.

I was tired after my speedy journey from Mount Nebo and had had little time and quiet to absorb that experience, so I left the company early. It was Barnabas and Mark's last evening and I did not want, as a stranger, to intrude on their last evening together with those of the Way. Perhaps, too, some there would remember me and the old uncertainties and suspicions would be aroused and I could not expect Ananias to help to restore their confidence in me on that occasion. I retired to my room and lay awake thinking of young Mark. I remembered his slightly anxious look of disbelief and realised that I must not expect to be easily accepted by those who had been close to Jesus in the flesh. Next morning Ananias told me that he had told Barnabas my story and Barnabas had questioned him closely about me. I was a little sorry that Ananias would have told him of that hot-headed, impatient Saul, for, though he had always had faith in me, he did not yet really know this new man, Paul, who had come back from Arabia. I had left Damascus under such a cloud of suspicion that, although Ananias had always seen me through Love's eyes, Barnabas might link me with the persecutions and horrors of which he had learnt in Jerusalem. Even Ananias does not yet know how different I am now from that old Saul. I soon fell asleep and when I rose in the morning and joined them I found Barnabas and Mark had gone. They had left before dawn.

My first Sabbath back in Damascus is ended. I received the warmth and welcome that I longed for from many of the brethren, some of whom I had met before and some who had more recently come from Jerusalem. When we stood in silence together, hands raised to receive Love's blessing, I was, as we all were, deeply aware of the Christ in the midst of us. In converse with our Lord, Jesus, and in his love for us we were united in peace.

I was also aware that there were still some there who found it hard to, and some who could not, receive me. They remembered the old Saul, impetuous, impatient, who had expected to be totally understood and instantly accepted among them when he turned so suddenly from persecutor to brother. I had been so hasty and insensitive. I had not understood and had been so aggrieved by their distrust. I could understand it now and when one of them turned away and would not meet me I longed to throw my arms around him and when I saw a small group that looked towards me and turned their backs and talked together, I sensed a grave distrust that verged on hostility. They saw me through mortal eyes and Love could not see Paul, beloved of Jesus, through their eyes, for they were spiritually blinded by their fear.

When Sabbath was over Ananias and I walked down to the stream where I had been baptised. "Well, Saul?" He queried, forgetting that after my baptism I had asked him to use my Greek name as a symbol that service of my Master would be among Gentiles more than Jews. I told him of the fear I had felt. "It will take time, Saul," he said. "The synagogue here is a very traditional group and we are anxious not to alienate ourselves from the others. By the power of the Holy Spirit of Jesus we must win them, especially the elders, to believe with us that he is alive and the power of Love, which is Messiah, is risen among us. You cannot hurry the work of Love. As yeast in flour It must work among us. Is it not this, above all, that Jesus showed us in those last days, when, step by step and moment by moment, unhurried, he went to the cross? He could so easily have chosen another way and demanded justice and we would have rallied round him. He, who spoke so eloquently, so fluently, could have called us to him and been the Messiah we expected. Many people were waiting to rally to his call and many of those closest to him were ready to draw swords in support of liberation. The Zealots longed for him. The Essenes claimed him. Every political party or eccentric fanatic saw in him the leader through whom victory and freedom could be won for their cause. Only some of us caught glimpses of the cause that was truly his — the single-minded love of the Father of all, Love Itself and through that, his love for us all, Love's children." He paused. We walked on in silence. Then he continued:

"Strangely enough it was his silence before the authorities, in those last hours, that revealed this to us more than his eloquence. His last words when he had been alone with us, before that awful arrest on the Mount of Olives, seemed to bind us together to support him more than anything else. They were not the last words of a man before his death. No Saul, he was not under any law of justice but only of Love and Love has nothing to say in self-defence. Love can only be lived and Jesus unswervingly lived it and from that came all that he suffered. So came his crucifixion. It needs time, Saul, and will take time, from now to eternity, for us to live and love as he did and prove, as he did, that sin, which in the eyes of the Law, is death, in the eyes of Love and in the sight of God, is understood and forgiven and we are freed from its slavery. It is because it has no power that he is alive. Messiah has come amongst us. Some among us, mostly the learned and scholarly ones, are re-reading the prophets and beginning to recognise that all they foretold has, in fact, been fulfilled by the life and death and resurrection of Jesus. In truth he is Messiah."

I was silenced by his wisdom. They had learnt in Damascus what I had learnt in Arabia, differently but just as convincingly. We came back, speaking no more to each other, but well aware that our hearts were on fire with love of the Christ within us who walked with us in the Way.

I have had several weeks in Damascus and they have not been easy. How far away and long ago seem those tremendous days of learning in Gadara, Pella, Jerash and the roads and camps in between and, finally, on Mount Nebo where horizons had opened to me and I had seen the whole world full of and hungering for Love.

Now my Lord is showing me the hard side of loving. Not for nothing have I realised that at the heart of my understanding is Jesus Christ crucified — dead to the mortal, dead to time and space and alive in the spirit and to eternity. Ultimate pain and suffering hung and died on that cross and that is the Way of Love on earth which I am now learning. I am being shunned, scorned, misunderstood, misinterpreted, not just by the elders, but by even some of the lovers of Jesus and true followers of the Way, children of our Father, Love, my own brothers. They do not see me through my lover's eyes as he sees me, in my Maker's image. They are still trying to hold the Law alongside Love and, blinded by my old sins, they cannot forgive me. They see Saul, hating, arrogant, uncertain, jealous and scornful and heap these things on the new Paul. They cannot see that they have transferred that same pride, arrogance, scorn, and even jealousy and fear, onto themselves.

I have learnt, with my beloved brothers here who see me through Love's eyes, to 'pray' to our Father God. This is very different from the solitary converse that I hold, moment by moment, with my Lord, which is an awareness of Messiah, among us and in each of us. In his resurrection body he is incarnate among us and we are made one in his name. I, who cover so much parchment with words and speak so freely, feel, when with my brethren, the danger of words. They are so limited and constraining, so easily misunderstood as to be divisive. The Word, the deep Logos, as the Greeks strive to understand it, is the Truth as many words can never be. Neither can words unite us in understanding as Love can. How can I help the brethren who suspect me to see me in Love? One young man, a new refugee from Jerusalem, when we were speaking of the division I was causing, said laughingly, that he remembers Jesus one day, sitting outside a villager's house watching a fussy hen calling her chickens to come under her wings and he said, "How often do I call you to me like that and you take no notice!"

He then said, "We will never do better than Jesus did, Paul! Many people turned away from him. We must be ready for the same rejection."

He comforted me but did not satisfy me.

A week ago things came to a head. Those Jews who had from the beginning been distrustful of me became suspicious and finally banded together in open hostility. I had been invited to speak in the synagogue last Sabbath and I said that though I might have scholarly knowledge, be a stern upholder of the Law, speak many languages, preach eloquently, do all manner of good deeds, give generously, even be ready for my body to be killed for my faith, it was all meaningless and empty without Love — the Love that is neither proud nor impatient but sees always in faith and hope, the perfect and eternal in his brother. It was too much for them.

Over Jordan

Two nights ago Ananias came to me after I had turned in for the night. I had retired early for I was bruised and aching and my back was sore for I had been attacked by a rough gang of Jewish students from the synagogue after Sabbath had ended.

"Brother Saul," he said, "you must leave Damascus quickly. The group here which beat you up and which has caused you such distress has finally convinced the elders that you are truly a follower of Jesus and that, while our own faith in him is difficult enough for them to handle, your seemingly casual attitude to the Law and reports of your meeting with Gentile families in Damascus make you as much a blasphemer and law-breaker in their eyes as ever Jesus was. There is a plot, led by one Simon bar Ephraim, to kill you. It was he who sent the gang which attacked you. Brother Saul, for the peace of us here and for you to be saved for your calling to the work of which you have spoken so often, you must go."

I had known of this group's hostility for some time but gave it little thought for my days were filled proving to those of the Way that I was truly one of them in love and that Ananias' and Judas' trust in me was not misplaced. Each day more brethren became reassured and accepting of me and our joy in our recognition of love and of the risen Christ among us and the power of his spirit had pushed any anxieties or thought of hostility from my mind.

I gathered my things together hastily and Ananias' young servant boy, Benji, was waiting to carry
them for me. "He and his cousin will travel with you
as far as Jordan river," Ananias said. "They will go
out by the South Gate with your goods when it is
opened in the morning. It is not safe for you to wait
until then, or go that way, for your persecutors may
well be in wait for you."

He led me in the dark to a narrow alley which
went behind the shops and houses through to the
city wall about three minutes walk from the main
gate. We climbed a stone stairway against the wall
to a door which led into a two-roomed house built
high into the wall. We entered. Opposite was a
wooden-shuttered door, bolted and barred, that
opened out from the wall, There was a strong smell
of fish in the room and a small oil-lamp was burning
and in its light I saw three men who greeted me by
name. "Brother Saul," they said and Ananias told
me that they were fishermen who were to help me to
escape. The tax collectors allowed fishermen to leave
the city by this door in the city wall, issuing them
with a pass for their return through customs next
day. They were to lower me through the window in a
basket used for bringing fish back from the river to
the market in the city. They would regularly leave
the city to fish by night with their baskets contain-
ing only their nets. Then, when the South Gate
opened at dawn they would return with their catch
and bring the fish in for market.

The men descended by a rope ladder and the
baskets were on a pulley, both of which could be
pulled up when out of use so that the city was
secured again. The man who lived in the wall was a

guard appointed especially to control the fishermen's departure and he was a follower of Jesus in
the Way. All went as they had planned. Once I had
reached the ground and the fishermen had joined me
it was safe for me to leave the basket and they led
me to a small lodge in a cultivated vegetable plot
and told me to wait until the boys joined me with my
loads when the gate opened at dawn. Here I can see,
through the dark, shapes of travellers, their camels
and mules, arriving to await the dawn opening of
the gate. I hear camel bells and donkey bells, the
bleating of sheep and goats, the creak of a few cart-
wheels, the shouts of drivers as they choose a plot of
ground to camp and await the dawn.

Things have moved so quickly for me that when
the men moved off for their fishing and left me I
could hardly believe what had happened were it not
for a powerful smell of fish in my cloak and the fish-
scales clinging to it. How easily I could have been
tracked down if anyone had expected my departure
that way! I have left Damascus. I am outside her
walls and after all these months, now years, I am
about to cross the Jordan river en route to Jerusalem. No more delays. I, Saul, am now truly Paul,
Ambassador of Love, servant of his Lord, Jesus. I am
nothing and yet I have all things. Yet I have never
felt so bruised, despised, rejected. My back is sore
and my bruises ache. I feel wretched and unhappy
and can only lean, helplessly, on my Lord, trust
myself to him and wait for the dawn.

During these hours of waiting the faces of those
who refuse to recognise me rise up before me
sneering, scornful and proud. I have deserved their
suspicion and scorn for I have been a persecutor of
the innocent, a turn-coat and finally a rebel, it

seemed, against the Law. Yet, had they truly known the Lord Jesus and believed in the Christ in me they would not have continued to judge and condemn me by the Law. I long to write to them but have no more paper with me until the boys join me in the morning.

As soon as the gate was opened this morning traffic moved freely in and out of the city and soon the boys found me. They had brought a donkey, for Ananias had told them that I might not be strong enough to walk. However, my wounds are healing swiftly except for bruises and a few deep scars, so we set off at once for the road under Hermon to the south. Though that road is familiar to me now I was glad of the boys' company and of the donkey to carry my load.

We are in my revelation wadi for I decided we would camp here for the night and it is in the firelight here that I have just written to the congregation in Damascus. I wanted to tell them that Love's understanding has forgiven us all and that love is shed abroad in our hearts by Christ Jesus, our resurrected Lord. We are one body with different parts and when each part works as it should the whole body grows in health and in love. I have told them I was sad to leave them before we had found peace together, that they only understood me in part and I longed for the day when we would all know and accept and understand each other as Jesus knew, understood and loved each of us. I begged them to learn as I am learning, to serve Love unafraid, knowing human judgement is bound to the Law and true freedom is only found through the

Love that we learn in Christ, our Lord, for that Love
fulfils all the Law and the prophesies,

Not until I had written that letter could I turn my
thoughts to this hallowed spot, the most precious
spot on earth to me. Now I wait, at peace, listening
to the quiet water breaking round the rocks.

Dawn has broken. I see the stream, the stony slopes
on either side, the willows and olive trees and an
oleander by the water. Because it is late spring-time
tiny marigolds, scarlet anemones and white daisies
gleam among lavender and rosemary, their colours
intensifying as daylight increases. Sadness, failure,
pain have left me and I am held in peace. It is very
still. Even the water seems to whisper. Nothing
strains for life. Effortlessly all things grow, never
earning their place in creation but accepting,
accepted and content. They never wrestle with each
other for supremacy but each gives its self and takes
its place with grace and humility. Have these tiny
plants flowered at my feet every spring-time and I
have been unaware? Is each created thing illuminated by the eyes of the Spirit? I picked a small
anemone bud and spread apart its collar of green
and opened its petals, folded, deep crimson, against
its heart and as I did so the sun shone on the flowers
and a small breeze made them shiver as it passed
over. Then stillness and peace again and I marvel,
for my eyes have never sensed in this way before,
the wonder of creation. The psalmist's words came to
me, "What is man that Thou art mindful of him?"
Love laughs and holds me close. The last time I was
here Love blinded me. This time Love has opened

my eyes. The tempestuous, proud Saul is dead. Paul is risen from the dead, in Christ alive for evermore.

The boys are still asleep, wrapped in their cloths. They and I, the earth and all created things are enfolded and one in the glory of God, the Father. All life is one, created by Love. This Power, that made the universe, is in me, in the flower in my hand, in these young boys sleeping at my feet, in the stars, the waning moon, in the night sky and the rising sun heralding in the new day. When we come together, in loving groups, we then also recognise one Lord, one God and Father of all, above all and through all and in us all.

Yet my Damascus experience in these last weeks has shown me, too, how hard it is to love. It can be thought about, talked about, recognised, but to love in every moment − that is hard. Often, still, my own judgement can rise, dominate and dictate and I see my fellow-men through the eyes of the Law as I have been trained to do and not through the eyes of Love Who loves the creature made in the image of the Creator. This has been my mistake in Damascus − mistake, not failure. This is why I have had to leave in haste. I saw the traditionalists through my own eyes and in judgement − as they also saw me − and this is the old way of the Law and not of Love. Will my letter help to put this right? We are all members of one Body, under Jesus, Messiah, our head. This is for ever true and when we are in disharmony we deny the Love that has freed us from the Law.

The boys are awake and unpacking the food Ananias has sent with them. I must join them for I will send them back to-day to deliver my letter to the chief priest of the synagogue.

This is my last entry in my journal. To-day I will join the crowds, cross over the river and make my way on foot to Jerusalem. My way has been made clear. I am, for the rest of my life, Love's ambassador to the world, in the service of Jesus, Lord, lover, working and longing for his Kingdom to be established on earth as it already is in heaven.

Over two years ago the wild, young rabbi, Saul, crossed over Jordan. Now, a new man, Paul, is crossing back. No longer am I the apparently zealous fanatic, with neither confidence nor goal, whose enthusiasm covered guilt and uncertainty. I am ambassador and apostle. My body, strong, alive and part of my humanity, is in subjection to the Holy Spirit of Love whose servant and lover I am, for it is not I but Christ who lives through me.

When the boys and I had eaten together they prepared to set off on their way back. They had hoped to come with me as far as the river but I told them that the speedy delivery of my letter was more important. Soon they were both mounted on the donkey trotting briskly away.

They have turned the corner and are out of sight and I realise there is no more looking back. From this holy spot I will again set out, knowing this time my high calling. A hoopoe has flown down tossing his crest; a bulbul sings in the bushes; the flowers open to the sun and I am silent in a peace past understanding.

A little slowly and reluctantly but firmly I have packed my things. My journal and writing materials are soon to be added and all will be slung over my shoulder and I will set out. I give thanks for all that has made me, for all my yesterdays, their discipline and learning and for the privilege of my calling.

Before me I see in the sunrise my risen Lord and behind that radiance the shadow of his thorn-crowned body on the cross. In that strength I go over Jordan to conquer the world for Love.

Appendix

The Dream

There is war in Heaven between Good and Evil, Light and Darkness. I am caught in that warfare, not knowing for which side I fight. I am fully armed with breast-plate, helmet with plume, sword and shield and legs girded. Philacteries are bound on my brow and arm. I have energy, strength and will, physical and spiritual, as never before.

I am astride a mighty charger which rears and thrusts so that I can barely hold or keep my seat. Never was there a greater or more powerful warrior than I and never has a braver soldier gone to war. Yet I know not on which side I fight. At one moment I am one with the hosts of Darkness. I strike out against the Light. This way and that I turn, obliterating from the dark the beams of light only for them to reappear in lightning flashes above and behind me. Darkness surges and seethes and masses. I am caught in its folds. I am absorbed in the shapeless, overwhelming immensity of its power. All my energy is used in the destruction of Light as I wrestle in the clutches of Darkness.

Suddenly I turn and flay and hack at the dark, caught in a brilliant beam of pure Light, empowered by It, filled with It. It flashes from my armour and my sword and I know It will never be overcome, however immense and overwhelming seems the

192

Dark. Again, I am fighting against the Light but never wounded, never overcome, always full of power and strength.

From time to time in my dream I fall into a great silence, back on my sleeping-mat, under the desert sky. I pull my blanket from my face and gaze and gaze into the night sky, dark and deep and yet always presaging dawn. Stars sparkle, silent, unafraid, and I gaze until I sleep again.

I am back on that battle-field. Light and Dark are locked in eternal warfare and I am fighting. I am victorious, first over Light and then over Darkness. I, the victor, on whichever side I fight.

Again I fall into that silence. I gaze into the sky, uncertain now, knowing no man can win a victory for both sides in any conflict. Then, suddenly, my eyes fall to the east and I see the first pearly gleam of dawn creeping over the horizon. The light of a new day is coming into the world. Darkness can only slink away, beaten back by the Light, overcome by Its power and glory. I have no thoughts, no words and, even now, have neither thoughts nor words about my dream. It happens to me and I happen in it.

Plato understood the battle of my dream, for he knew which of the worlds in which we live is shadow and which is substance, where is Darkness and where is Light. I know that my hunger and longing is to fight a good fight, to live to the full in freely chosen service, to be unfettered by man-made law or tradition, to love to the uttermost, unbound and unafraid. This is the battle of my dream.